D1521972

A COMPREHENSIVE VIEW
OF FREEMASONRY

**Presented by
Paola Masonic Lodge No. 37
Ancient Free and Accepted
Masons of Kansas**

OTHER BOOKS BY
THE AUTHOR

Outlines of Freemasonry (1939)

The History of Liberty (1965)

Coil's Masonic Encyclopedia (1961)
Revised edition (1996)

Freemasonry Through Six Centuries,
2 Volumes (1967)

"Masonic Fraternity" in the
Encyclopedia Americana

A Comprehensive View of Freemasonry

by

HENRY WILSON COIL, 33⁰

CHAIRMAN, COMMITTEE ON MASONIC INFORMATION,
GRAND LODGE F. & A.M. OF CALIFORNIA

Revised edition based on latest data in
Coil's Masonic Encyclopedia
Revised edition of 1996.

MACOY PUBLISHING & MASONIC SUPPLY CO., INC.
Richmond, Virginia

Contents

List of Illustrations

Revised Edition of 1998

A revised edition of the book which continues to receive highest praise world wide for its analytical coverage of the entire scope of the Rise and Development of Freemasonry from earliest time. Mr. Coil's legalistic background, his love for Masonic history and extensive research have divested the Fraternity of its antequated legends, yet honoring the importance of its allegiance to its allegorical teachings.

The book was first published in 1973. Mr. Coil died January 29, 1974 and important changes in the world have taken place which need to be incorporated in this lasting and worthy contribution of Masonic literature.

Prominent Freemasons have graciously contributed such additions to this revision — among them Bishop Carl J. Sanders, the late Norman Vincent Peale, D.D., Forrest D. Haggard, D.D., the late Allen E. Roberts — and others. Their contributions are mainly in the articles on *Black Freemasonry, Mormonism, Catholicism, Religion and European Freemasonry since World War II.*

Printed in Enlarged Type.

Preface

HE PURPOSE of this book is to give a brief but comprehensive view of Free masonry from the earliest historical record of it to the present day, and to correlate and explain its development in various times and places as it spread from the British Isles over the world. This work does not, and cannot, in the limited space occupied, purport to be a history, though it is believed that no important event has been omitted, and the chronology of occurrences is fairly well defined. It may, therefore, serve as an index for further investigation and enable the reader better to see the relation, which any other work he happens to read bears to the whole subject.

It must be borne in mind that Masonic books of all kinds were coming off the presses for more than a century before the first dependable and complete history of Freemasonry was published in 1885, and that less than three-quarters of a century has not been sufficient to remove the errors put in circulation by such earlier works, some of which are still read. For that reason, it has been deemed helpful to review in opening pages the general nature and scope of Masonic historiography and literature so as to point out when and how various concepts arose, and, thus, to enable the reader to judge their degree of authenticity.

The author acknowledges his indebtedness to M. W. Bro. Charles C. Hunt of the Grand Lodge of Iowa and M. W. Bro. Wm. Rhodes Hervey of the Grand Lodge of California and Sovereign Grand Inspector General, both now deceased, and to W. Bro. Harold V. B. Voorhis, 33', of New Jersey for their helpfulness and advice over many years in the intricacies of Masonic research and writings.

HENRY WILSON COIL, A.B., LL.B.

Riverside, California,
October, 1952

CHAPTER 1

Introduction

HE FREEMASONS, variously called the Ancient and Honorable Society of Free and Accepted Masons, Ancient Free and Accepted Masons, Masonic Fraternity, or simply Masons, is beyond question the oldest, the most numerous, the most widely dispersed, and the most curious of all secular societies. Questions concerning its origin and the history, nature, and meaning of its ceremonies have attracted the attention of the closest students and the most indefatigable antiquaries, without completely satisfactory answers. As the survival of the mediaeval fraternity of builders, architects, artisans, and artists, the order can be traced back about five centuries to a time when, though then suffering decay from the decline in Gothic construction, it possessed and preserved legends of a much earlier origin, which have been the inspiration for many efforts at enlargement, illustration, and embellishment.

Some of the legends and most of the principles and behests contained in the earliest records of the Fraternity, i.e. the Gothic Constitutions, have been adhered to with remarkable consistency, even into the present era, and, notwithstanding the lapse of time and the changes in social structure, have drifted but slightly from their original import, and then only reluctantly. Though the Society has experienced many vicissitudes and been subjected to many stresses, particularly, in being transplanted from its original habitat in Britain into many lands and among various peoples, though its control and administration have been loose, never unified under a single authority, and though its symbolism and ceremonies have been expanded and embellished, and, at times, supplemented by new themes woven into the fabric, yet, due to a persistent distaste for innovations, which seems to have animated its votaries from the first, its fundamental character, philosophy, purposes, tenets, and customs have remained remarkably true to the original stock.

Never having possessed a hierarchy of any sort but having been from the first a brotherhood bound together by ties of amity, its government has become increasingly dispersed and varied as it has crossed national and state lines, until it's administration at the present day is shared by approximately one hundred Grand Lodges in as many political nations, states, and subdivisions. Hence, though generally referred to as a society or order, and though Freemasons everywhere recognize a mystic tie, the whole can hardly be called an organization, a corpus, or an entity, but rather must be considered a group of independent units adhering in the main to the same doctrine, laws, and customs, inculcating nearly the same truths by the same or like symbols and ceremonies, and exhibiting the same general appearance and character.

Therefore, what is called the Society or Fraternity of Freemasons is more in the nature of a system of philosophy or of moral and social virtues taught by symbols, allegories, and lectures based upon fundamental truths, the observance of which tends to promote stability of character, conservatism, morality and good citizenship. Moderation and toleration are so respected that differences of opinion among its members, even about its policies and purposes, are permitted quite as much as those about extraneous matters. The Society does not proselyte but, in accordance with time-honored custom, insists that each applicant come of his own free will and accord. It has no program or propaganda of political, religious, or social reform, and it is singularly self-contained, especially refraining from political and religious embroilment, and even declining association with other societies and movements, no matter how beneficent their immediate objectives may appear.

To the difficulty of understanding the original or main stem of Freemasonry, called Craft Masonry or Blue Masonry, comprising the three degrees of Entered Apprentice, Fellow Craft and Master Mason, under the government of Grand Lodges, there is added the complication of numerous so-called higher degrees and orders which have been gradually imposed upon or appended to it, beginning in the early 18th century and continuing into recent years. Besides the four quite extensive bodies, known as Royal Arch Masons, Royal and Select Masters, Knights Templar, and the Scottish Rite, embracing in the aggregate about forty degrees, some of them remarkably elaborate and otherwise differing from the basic rite, there have been accumulating over the years in the United States, and to a less degree elsewhere, no less than three dozen other orders, all confining their memberships to Master Masons, to which must be added several orders for women, girls, and boys who are related to Master Masons.

Due to a widespread belief which permeated Masonic thought up to the last half of the 19th century, that Freemasonry had, from ancient times, at least from the reign of King Solomon, embraced the three degrees and no more and, hence, that, under the doctrine of the immutability of Masonry, it could suffer no addition, Grand Lodges have generally refused to recognize those higher degrees as Masonic, though notable exceptions exist, especially in Scandinavian and Latin countries. But, just as common understanding or misunderstanding in any field often ignores technical distinctions, most of these higher degrees and orders are, in the common parlance of Freemasons, as well as of the public, considered not only Masonic but as the very flower of Masonry, and they are often administered by the same individuals who hold the highest offices in the more restricted Grand Lodges. The term, Freemasonry, therefore, is used loosely, within and without the Fraternity, to include practically all bodies composed of Master Masons, though bearing distinctive names, conferring degrees, and pursuing policies differing from those of the Blue Lodges.

Lack of discrimination between the basic Craft Rite and the numerous accretions to it often characterizes writings, which endeavor to define and explain Freemasonry, so that the difficulty of determining whether the one or the other is referred to leads to obscurity and error

[5]

and tends to break down those very distinctions which Grand Lodges insist upon. Hence, the term, Freemasonry, has been made broader and less exact and its definition has been rendered almost impossible. While many have offered aphorisms or metaphors about Freemasonry, no one has heretofore succeeded in formulating a definition of it which is mutually inclusive and exclusive, and, of all who have attempted it, the most erudite are no less enigmatic than the others.

CHAPTER II

Historiography and Literature

NO VEHICLE of thought has had so many "hitch-hikers" aboard as has the literature of Freemasonry, many having distorted its history or added grotesque themes to its simple, ethical, and moral doctrine. Because imaginative and often preposterous writings of innumerable authors have had an unavoidable and sometimes unfortunate effect in shaping concepts of Freemasonry, both within and without the Fraternity, it is advisable to treat, first and out of the usual order, the causes and development of these ideas.

The literature of the subject is quite extensive, it being asserted that more books have been written upon it than upon any other. The more pretentious historiographic and analytical works possibly number 500 to 600, but Wolfstieg's *Bib-*

liography lists 80,000 titles of Masonic books of all kinds in Europe alone, to which probably 20,000 in America must be added. Such numbers include, however, Grand Lodge proceedings, lodge histories, brochures, privately printed works and others of local or transient importance only. One Masonic library breaks the whole subject matter into 3,000, and another into 4,000 sub-heads. But many "Masonic" books are such only in the opinions of their authors.

Much so-called Masonic writing has been worthless or misleading. No work published prior to 1860 upon the historical phase is of any value whatever, and many of earlier or later dates upon symbolism and philosophy are quite undependable. Error in the former class arose from the failure of authors to make any investigation of facts about the origin of the Society, carelessness and imagination having full play. As for the latter class, chance or insignificant resemblance between the symbols and ceremonies of Freemasonry and those of ancient times led to unwarranted and often absurd conclusions. Masonry has neither censor of books nor any official agency for the dissemination of information about itself, and full advantage has been taken of that liberty, provoking Hallam (*Middle Ages*, 1818-48, Vol. III p. 359) to exclaim:

"The curious subject of Freemasonry has been treated of only by panegyrists or calumniators, both equally mendacious."

A Masonic literature can hardly be said to have existed prior to the latter half of the 18th century, and the light which might otherwise be cast upon the critical half century following the establishment of the first symbolic Grand Lodge in 1717 is regrettably lacking.

It was the invariable practice of all writers, prior to the American Civil War, to trace the origin of the Fraternity to remote ages of the past. This is undoubtedly attributable to the fact that the Gothic Constitutions contained legends which gave credit to Juball, son of Lamech, who lived before the Flood, for the invention of Masonry or Geometry, the two being treated as synonymous, and recounted the participation of Masons in the erection of the Tower of Babel and of King Solomon's Temple, all of which fancy was greatly expanded and particularized by Dr. James Anderson in a preface to the *Constitutions* adopted by the Grand Lodge of England in 1723. This fabulous tale, exceeded in absurdity only by the revision of it in the second edition of those *Constitutions* in 1738 by the same author, gravely stated, among other things, that

"the Israelites, at their leaving Egypt, were a whole Kingdom of Masons, well instructed, under the Conduct of their

Grand Master Moses, who often marshall'd them into a regular and general Lodge, while in the Wilderness, * * * the wise King Solomon was Grand Master of the Lodge at Jerusalem, and the learned King Hiram was Grand Master of the Lodge at Tyre * * * Kings, Princes, and Potentates built many glorious Piles and became Grand Masters, each in his own Territory, * * * the Grand Monarch Nebuchadnezzer * * * became the Grand Master-Mason * * * Zerubbabel the Prince and General Master-Mason of the Jews, * * * Ptolomeus Philadelphus became an excellent Architect and General Master-Mason * * * the glorious Augustus became the Grand Master of the Lodge at Rome."

In the second edition, the *Constitutions* of 1738, Dr. Anderson exceeded his former effort, conferring Grand Masterships upon figures previously overlooked, adopting the office of Provincial Grand Master and filling that too with personages of slightly lower worldly rank, and so offending fact and reason that it now scarcely, seems possible that he was in earnest. But he was taken seriously by possibly a majority of the Craft, certainly by its literary contingent, which followed that general approach to the subject for more than a century.

The first fifty years of symbolic or Grand Lodge Masonry brought forth, in addition to the *Constitutions* above mentioned, only the following: a score of pretended exposes of the ritual and secrets, a dozen preserved lectures and sermons, and two books.

The exposes, doubtless discomforting to the young Grand Lodge, are invaluable to the modern student in exposing, quite as much as they did to the public in earlier times, the working of lodges in the pre-Grand Lodge era, and possibly extending into the following era. These began almost immediately upon the accession of the new regime; *A Mason's Examination* in 1723; *The Grand Mystery of Freemasons Discover'd* in 1724; *The Secret History of Freemasonry* in 1724; *Briscoe* MS. in 1724-25; *The Freemason's Accusation and Defense* in 1726; *A Mason's Confession* in 1727; *Masonry Dissected* in 1730; *The Secrets of Masonry Made Known to All Men* in 1737; *The Mystery of Masonry* in 1737; *Masonry Further Dissected* in 1738; *Le Secrets des Franc-Macons* in 1742; *Catechisme des Franc-Macons* in 1745; *L'Ordre de Franc-Macons trahe et le Secret Mopses revele* in 1745; *Le Macon demasque* in 1751; *A Master Key to Freemasonry* in 1760; *Three Distinct Knocks* in 1760; *Jachin and Boaz* in 1762; *Hiram, the Grand Master Key* in 1764; *Shibboleth or Every Man a Freemason* in 1765; *Solomon in all his Glory* in 1766; *Mahabone or the Grand Lodge Door Opened* in 1766; *Tubal-Kain* in 1767; and *The Freemason Stripped Naked* in 1769; to which many more were added later.

The two books were Smith's *Pocket Companion*, a manual, in 1735 and Fifield Dassigny's *A Serious and Impartial Enquiry into the Cause of the Present Decay of Freemasonry in the Kingdom of Ireland*, published in Dublin in 1744, the only important feature of which is its mention of the Royal Arch, the earliest known reference to that degree.

Ten Masonic addresses between 1721 and 1765 are preserved, which indicate that the doctrinal feature of Freemasonry was serious, moral, virtuous, and uplifting, but that its symbolism and philosophy were yet to experience considerable development. Two of these addresses were epochal and of far reaching consequence.

In 1730, Martin Clare, later to become Junior Grand Warden and Deputy Grand Master, delivered his *Defense of Masonry* in response to Samuel Prichard's *Masonry Dissected* of the same year, in which it had been charged that Freemasonry was a "ridiculous imposition," a "pernicious society," and both" a wicked fraud" and "an unintelligible heap of stuff and jargon, without common sense or connection." Refusing to admit or deny anything about the secrets of Freemasonry, but expressly assuming that everything said about them was true, Clare then proceeded to show that Masonry was still a permissible and worthwhile moral and social diversion. The jargon, he said, was in no essential respect different from that found in Ecclesiastes 12: 3-6; that much more could be found which resembled the hieroglyphics of the Egyptians, the discipline of the Pythagoreans, the practices of the Essenes, the mysteries of the Cabalists, the ceremonies of the Druids, and several myths and legends of classical writings; and that he was apt to think that

"Masonry, as it is now explained, has in some circumstances declined from its original purity. It has run long in muddy streams, and, as it were, underground; but notwithstanding the great rust it may have contracted, and the forbidding light in which it is placed by the dissector, there is still much of the old fabric remaining; the essential pillars of the building may be discovered through the rubbish, though the superstructure be overrun with moss and ivy, and the stones, by length of time, be disjointed,"

Whatever may have been the justification for these deductions, the classical references which Clare thus expressed pointed in several of the directions trod by later writers and added to the rather trite Andersonian theme just the proper flavor of myth, mysticism, and paganism to open the vista upon all of the philosophies and religions of ancient times.

Seven years later, the Chevalier Andrew Michael Ramsay added another touch in his now celebrated address or charge (Gould, *History of Freemasonry*, Vol. III, p. 338) in a lodge at Paris,

March 21,1737. Ramsay was a Scotsman, educated in the University of Edinburgh, later a tutor in several noble families, including that of the Pretender, James III, and converted to the Roman Catholic faith by Fenelon, Archbishop of Cambrai. In 1737, Ramsay bore the title of Grand Chancellor of some Masonic body at Paris, but his prior Masonic activities are unknown. His address was a panegyrical and pretended historical account of the descent of Freemasonry from the Crusades, thus, substituting, for what to the French mind was a lowly architectural and operative background, a more impressive, chivalric, and knightly ancestry. The secrets of Freemasonry, said he, included the pass words of the military camps in Palestine, and the Order, founded in remote antiquity, united with the Knights of St. John of Jerusalem, following the example set by the Israelites in the erection of the Second Temple, who, whilst "they handled the trowel and mortar in one hand, in the other held the sword and buckler." He said that the lodges then located throughout Europe and the British Isles were founded by kings and princes upon their return from the Crusades; that James, Lord Steward of Scotland, was Grand Master of a lodge at Kilwinning in A.D. 1286, and Prince Edward (Edward I), son of Henry III, brought his troops back from the last Crusade, established them in England as a colony of brothers, and declared himself protector of the Order, which had assumed the name, Freemasons, after the example set by their ancestors. He attributed the absence of earlier lodges in Europe to the religious discords of the 16th century, and recognized that Masonry from Britain was reentering France, which was to become the center of the Order. Ramsay also had recourse to the ancient mysteries, stating that the famous festivals of Ceres at Eleusis, of Isis in Egypt, of Minerva at Athens, of Urania amongst the Phoenicians, and of Diana in Scythia "were connected with ours," and that those mysteries concealed many vestiges of the ancient religion of Noah and the Patriarchs.

This brief and only appearance of Ramsay on the Masonic stage, though he lived six years beyond it, has aroused much speculation and many unjustified deductions as to his authorship of the Hauts Grades, but it is generally agreed to have been the inspiration for the higher degrees, the production of which was under way by 1740, profoundly affecting the literature and course of Freemasonry as later detailed.

Not until the last third of the 18th century was serious effort made to explain Freemasonry in book form. The first of these and what now seems as almost trivial treatment of the subject was published at London in 1769 by Wellins Calcott and entitled *A Candid Disquisition of the Principles and Practices of the Most Ancient and Honorable Society of Free and Accepted Masons, together with Some Strictures on the Origin, Nature, and Design of that Institution.* This was soon followed by William Preston's *Illustrations of Masonry* in 1772 and William Hutchinson's *Spirit of Masonry* in 1775, the latter being the first work to attempt an analysis and explanation of the spiritual and religious aspect of Freemasonry, urging its Patriarchal origin and its then Christian character and purposes.

By the close of the 18th century, the germs of the ideas implicit in the orations of 1730 and 1737 had sprouted and begun to grow as vines rampant, sending their canes and stems interwinding in strangely variant and intricate patterns, a growth which, though now slowed, has never entirely ceased. Ramsay's oration produced a considerable Templar-Masonic type of literature and gave rise to numerous degrees now included in the York Rite and the Scottish Rite. Together with the oration of Clare, they furnished the inspiration for an abundant literature of the "Ancient Mysteries" type. The latter was adopted by the Abbe Robin in his *Researches in Ancient and Modern Initiation,* (1779); by Paul J. S. Vogel in *Letters Concern-*

ing Freemasonry, (1785); by Osnabruck, (1789); and by Alexander Lenoir in *Freemasonry Traced to its True Origin or the Antiquity of Freemasonry Proved by Explication of Ancient and Modern Mysteries,* (1814). Strangely enough, British and American writers were most affected by the asserted coincidence of some symbols and ceremonies of the Masonic rituals with those of one or more ancient philosophies, religions, and mysteries, such as those of Osiris and Isis, Mithras, Bacchus, Eleusis, Adon, Venus and Adonis, the Cabiri, the Essenes, Dionysus, the Dionysian Artificers, the Druids, and the Culdees, sometimes mingled with Pythagorean, Hermetic, Alchemical, or Rosicrucian symbolism and vagaries. The hiatus of eighteen or twenty centuries between the ancient putative prototype and the more recent supposed descendant was blandly ignored.

No adequate review is possible of the great volume and ramifications of Masonic literature of the 19th century, probably its most luxuriant period. The two most prolific and influential writers of that era were Dr. George Oliver in England and Dr. Albert G. Mackey in the United States. The former, between 1820 and 1863, produced no less than two dozen works, his last appearing posthumously in 1875. Always a credulous victim of hearsay and misleading rumors, which he applied unhesitatingly, his works have no historical merit, being chiefly characterized by adherence to the Andersonian theory of patriarchal origin of the Society and its essential Christian character. His prestige, however, was wide and exerted considerable influence on American Literature.

Dr. Mackey's works are difficult to describe briefly, exploring, as they did, every phase of the subject, rituals, symbolism, law, and history. Some of his books, though later inferentially repudiated by himself, still circulate, and his *Encyclopaedia of Freemasonry*, with all its errors, contains so much valuable information that it remains the standard work of the kind in this country. He was neither a soulful nor a panegyrical writer, but being a physician, he dissected Freemasonry unfeelingly and dogmatically announced the results of his autopsy, which were received as conclusive by a large segment of the Craft. Mackey was made a Mason in 1841, and began his authorship only four years later. He underwent an experience to which few other productive authors were subjected in that he spent the first two-thirds of his literary career of thirty-six years under the spell of the Anderson-Preston-Oliver school and the last third torn between the realism of the Woodford-Hughan-Gould group and the exponents of ancient paganism, the latter then in its ascendancy, as indicated by the fact that, be-

Fac-simile from the original MS. of the Minute of the Admission to the Lodge of Edinburgh of Lord Alexander and Sir Anthonie Alexander, July 3, 1634.

Whereby the Craft might be
Slaundered. And also that no
fellow goe into the Town in
Night times without Two or
Three Witnesses with him—
Least the Trade be charge of
Villanie by him, to the griefe
of his fellows, without that
he haue a fellow with him.
that may bear him Witness
that he was in honest places.
Also that euery Master, and
fellow, shall come to the Assembly
if that it be within Fiftie
Milles about him, if he haue

tween 1856 and 1885, no less than a score of books appeared on that subject in England and America.

Albert Pike, one of the most profound students of ancient mysticisms, religions, and philosophies, and probably the greatest of this class of Masonic authors, was made a Mason in 1850, three years later being inducted by Mackey into the Scottish Rite and becoming Grand Commander of the Southern Jurisdiction of the United States in 1859. Pike seems never to have had any other concept of Masonry than that it was a descendant or a revival of the ancient mysteries, and he repeatedly expressed contempt for what he considered the puerilities of the Blue Lodge ritual. His ideas, encouraged by the popularity of the thesis at the time and confirmed by what he found in the rituals of the French Rite, Rite of Perfection, and the Scottish Rite, which he completely revised and enlarged, commencing in 1854, are to be found in *Morals and Dogma of the Ancient and Accepted Scottish Rite* (1871).

Though Pike was justified in emphasizing ancient mysticism in the Scottish degrees, Mackey was hardly excusable in carrying it into Blue Masonry and especially in pushing these ideas to the regrettable extremes to which he did in his *Masonic Ritualist* (1867) and *Symbolism of Freemasonry* (1869), the latter of which still circulates, revised but little purified, notwithstanding the author's retraction prior to his death in 1881. Shortly after that time, Mackey had shifted to the school of British realism, and, in his *History of Freemasonry,* written prior to 1881 and published posthumously in 1898 (Vol. I, pp. 185-197), reversed his former views on the pagan mysteries. This seems to indicate that, in Mackey's opinion at least, the ancient mystery theory of the origin of Masonic symbolism and ceremonies was untenable, being based solely on the assumption theretofore indulged that Freemasonry had its origin in the East in patriarchal times and was akin to, or derived from, other surrounding and contemporaneous societies and philosophies.

The early period referred to was 1500 to 2000 years prior to the first evidence we have of a fraternity of stonemasons or Freemasons, and, since there is nothing to bridge that great lapse of time and since neither the Gothic Constitutions nor the exposes of pre-Grand Lodge rituals contain material of a pagan mystical nature, the Pagan or Patriarchal origin of the Society was based on pure fancy. It is possible or even probable, however, that the ritualists of the Grand Lodge era drew on ancient sources for the elaboration and multiplication of the ceremonies, and that some such material was present by 1730 as indicated by Martin Clare's *Defense of Masonry.*

The Patriarchal origin as expressed by Anderson, Preston, Hutchinson, Oliver, Mitchell and others; the ancient pagan mystical theory advanced by the Abbe Robin, Paul J. S. Vogel, Osnabruck, Alexander Lenoir and others; and the Chivalric, Templar, or Crusader theme, first voiced by Ramsay in 1737, were the principal theses of the origin and antiquity of Freemasonry expressed by writers up to the third quarter of the 19th century. But there were minor and variant theses presented, so that, if the whole body of Masonic literature were examined, it will be found to contain at least twenty-five asserted origins of Freemasonry as follows:

(A) Patriarchal.

    (1) The Creation of the World; (2) King Solomon; (3) The Building of King Solomon's Temple; (4) The Patriarchal Religion; (5) Moses;

(B) Geometrical or Mathematical.

    (6) Euclid; (7) Pythagoras;

(C) Pagan or Mystical.

    (8) The Ancient Pagan Mysteries; (9) The Essenes; (10) The Culdees; (11) The Druids; (12) The Gypsies; (13) The Rosicrucians;

(D) Chivalric.

    (14) The Crusaders; (15) The Knights Templar;

(E) Political.
    (16) Oliver Cromwell; (17) The Pretender for the Restoration of the House of Stuart;

(F) Personal.
    (18) Lord Bacon; (19) Dr. Desaguliers and his associates in 1717;

(G) Trade Operative.
    (20) The Roman Collegia of Artificers;
    (21) The Comacine Masters; (22) The Steinmetzen; (23) The French Compagnons; (24) Sir Christopher Wren at the Building of St. Paul's Cathedral; and (25) The English and Scots stonemasons of the Middle Ages.

The concept, now almost universally entertained, that Freemasonry had its origin in the stonemasons' fraternity in the British Isles before the end of the 14th century and possibly as early as the 12th, developed but slowly. The operative origin was first suggested by German writers, who, however, naturally and as it appears erroneously, traced it back to the Steinmetzen. This idea was stumbled upon incidentally by the Abbe Grandidier in his preparation of an essay on Strassburg Cathedral in 1779, he having noticed the resemblance between the customs of the lodges of Freemasons and the Constitutions of the Steinmetzen (1459), the Torgau Ordinances (1462), and the Brother-Book (1563). The theme was developed by Paul J. S. Vogel in his *Letters Concerning Freemasonry,* (1785), which was the first attempt to investigate the early history of the Craft. This was followed by K. C. F. Krause's *The Three Oldest Professional Documents of the Brotherhood of Freemasons,* (1810); F. Heldmann's *The Three Oldest Memorials of the German Freemasonic Brotherhoods,* (1819); G. B. F. Kloss' *Freemasonry in its True Meaning* etc., (1846); F. A. Fallou's *The Mysteries of Freemasonry,* (1848); J. G. Findel's *History of Freemasonry from its Origin to the Present Day,* (1861); and G. W. Steinbrenner's *Origin and Early History of Freemasonry,* (New York, 1864).

Pioneering and commendable as their efforts were, the German writers had warning as early as 1840 that their plot might be true but that the scene was misplaced, for, in that year, J. O. Halliwell-Phillips, a non Mason, published his discovery of the nature of the Regius MS., which had lain in the British Museum disguised as a *Poem of Moral Duties.* Yet, twenty-nine years were to pass before the British Masons took the hint, during which period, the Germans reiterated their Steinmetzen thesis, culminating in Findel's work of 1861.

The British revolution in Masonic thought may be said to have occupied approximately the 16-year period from 1869 to 1885. William James Hughan, who had not been made a Mason until 1863, led it. In quick succession, he published his *Constitutions of the Freemasons,* (1869); *Masonic Sketches,* (1871) and *Old Charges of the British Freemasons,* (1872). In 1870, W. P. Buchan issued a series of articles opposed to the "revival" theory, i.e. that the Grand Lodge of 1717 was the revival of a prior similar body which had fallen into decay. In 1873, D. M. Lyon published his *History of the Lodge of Edinburgh.* Then came the exception to the general American apathy, with the publication in 1875 of George F. Fort's *Early History and Antiquities of Freemasonry as Connected with the Ancient Norse Guilds and the Oriental and Medieval Building Fraternities.* In 1878, Hughan issued his *Register of Lodges* and Robert Wylie, his *History of the Mother Lodge Kilwinning.* Then followed W. H. Rylands' *Freemasonry in the Seventeenth Century,* (1881); Fort's *Critical Inquiry into the Conditions of the Constitutional Builders and their Relations to Secular Guilds of the Middle Ages,* (1884) and *Historical Treatise on Early Builders' Marks*

(1885); and Hughan's *Origin of the English Rite of Freemasonry* (1884) and *Old Charges of the British Freemasons,* (2nd ed. 1895),

Meanwhile, Robert Freke Gould, who was destined to take foremost place among Masonic historians, began his contributions in 1879 with his *Atholl Lodges and Four Old Lodges.* His epochal and monumental *History of Freemasonry,* (1885), which completely superseded all prior works of the kind, has now, for more than half a century, been recognized as the premier authority upon the subject, notwithstanding some modifications and additions of details by later investigators. Gould, finding little plausibility in the efforts to link Freemasonry with ancient secret societies, notwithstanding that, in the thirty years preceding his work, no less than a score of books upon that theme had appeared in England and America, demolished the fanciful tales of Anderson, Preston, and Oliver, exposed the mistakes of Ramsay, Findel and others, and proceeded logically to demonstrate the rise of Freemasonry out of the English and Scots lodges of the 16th and prior centuries, supporting his conclusions by references to the Gothic Constitutions, lodge minutes, and other documents of unquestionable genuineness and authenticity. The subject was at last upon a true historiographic footing.

But Masonic literature may suffer from something resembling Bentham's law of money; the bad often drives the good out of the market, for, so widespread has been the effect of Pagan Mysticism and spurious "symbolism," particularly, on the public, that it is common to find in the book-stores works on Freemasonry on the same shelves with those on Theosophy, Astrology, Occultism, Alchemy, Hermeticism, Rosicrucianism, Asceticism, Magic, and Necromancy. It is necessary to observe in conclusion that the term, Masonic literature, is applied to everything that is written about Freemasonry by either those within or those without the Fraternity, by either those well informed or those not informed at all upon the subject, by either those who search for facts or those to whom facts are a tedious drag on imagination, and by either those who genuinely try to find out what Freemasonry is and those who are solely concerned with what they think it ought to be. How, then, can one know what is true and what is false; and how can one know when he is reading an authentic work and when not? The answer is: only by study and experience; by much the same process which renders the expert capable of pronouncing a stone a gem or a worthless imitation.

———•——◦◦—•———

CHAPTER III

Gothic Era

Gothic Architecture

RUE GENEALOGICAL RESEARCH, which should be applied to a society as well as to an individual, requires, not that the descendants of a putative ancestor be traced to find if the individual in question can be found among them, but that, beginning with the individual, we trace his ancestors back without prejudgment as to who may be found in the line of ascent. Applying that method, which has too often been neglected in Masonic investigation, we can trace Freemasonry from the present day back through the proceedings of various Masonic bodies to the premier Grand Lodge of England, thence, through scant lodge minutes and extraneous references in England and much more continuous minutes of lodges in Scotland to the year A.D. 1598, and thence, through the Gothic Constitutions in England, to the later 14th or early 15th century. In Germany, we find the Constitutions of the Steinmetzen of 1459, the Torgau Ordinances of 1462, and the Brother-Book of 1563, remarkably similar to the Charges of the British Freemasons, and, in France, we find the masons' fraternities, Les Compagnons du Tour de France, with legends bearing striking resemblance to the Legend of Hiram. While the Continental fraternities seem not to be in the line of ancestry, they are confirmatory of what we find in Britain in the way of builder-brotherhoods. All of them were occupied in a type of architecture called Gothic, though that is a misnomer, since the last Gothic kingdom perished several centuries before the first example of this style appeared.

Although all crafts and trades have had their peculiar "mysteries" and have them to this day, and although this was doubtless true of Greek, Roman, and Byzantine builders, who exhibited both artistry and skill, the fundamentals of their art seemed to involve no especial secret methods. Mechanically, there was required to be built into a wall, arch, or pier enough stone to absorb the stress to be placed upon it, to thicken a wall sufficiently to bear the lateral thrust from the adjacent arches, vault, or roof, wherefore the structure had the appearance of massive stability but suffered its usable room to be diminished by thick walls and large pillars, and was poorly lighted by the few, small windows deeply set in the thick walls. For a full understanding of Gothic architecture, reference must be made to specialized works. Here, it must suffice to say that it constituted a distinct departure and was easily distinguishable from all that had preceded it; its invention seems to have involved a flash of genius. A peculiarity of this style was that structural elements such as flying buttresses and groined vault ribs were not only exposed but also were made into decorative features.

The Gothic cathedral had the appearance of lightness and elevation, the whole presenting a lofty aspect, which was accentuated by pointed arches and quite often by spires in the order of 400 or more feet above the ground. The area occupied by walls and piers frequently did not exceed one-tenth of the ground area of the building, and the comparatively thin, high walls permitted vaulted ceilings sometimes 100 feet above the floor and were pierced by so many windows that some critics referred to them as "walls of glass with a roof of stone." A frequent jewel of the Gothic cathedral was the "rose window" of stained glass often 30 to 40 feet in diameter, placed above the entrance in the west end between the bases of the spires, the latter being sometimes left unfinished or intentionally truncated and left as turrets. One of the principal and most remarkable features consisted of the flying buttresses, which applied inward force at the tops of the walls to counteract the outward thrust of the vaults and stone-covered pitched roof. Such balancing of opposing forces, which today would be calculated by mathematical formula, was arrived at by the Freemasons in some manner as much a mystery to us as it was to the cowans, rough masons, wallers, and rubble workers of those times. Since books on mathematics, architecture, engineering, or physics did not exist, and since the consequences of miscalculation would have been ruinous, there is suggested the possibility that the proper relations were exemplified by models and their dimensions increased proportionately to give those of the finished structure, but this is mere surmise. Whatever explanation is offered must explain the simultaneous completion of the flying buttresses and the pitched roof so that neither would precipitate the wall before counteracted by the other.

Hence, there was more than ordinary craft mystery involved and, hence, the injunction (Harleian MS. No. 1942), "secure and keepe secret the obscure and intricate parts of the Science." Such policy may, at first blush, be deemed calculated to preserve a monopoly, but this is negatived by many other behests, such as those to do work truly and faithfully to the advantage of the Lord or owner, to take no work not within the capacity of the Mason so that no aspersion or discredit be imputed to the Science or that the owner be prejudiced. These indicate solicitude for the efficiency and reputation of the Craft much like that exhibited by the trade guilds, based on the concept that each workman was responsible for the products of every other workman and equally interested in its perfection.

Gothic came into being, matured, dominated the field, and died out in the relatively short period of about 400 years between the middle of the 12th and the middle of the 16th centuries. It was almost certainly invented in the Ile de France, between the Seine and the Marne, where the first example appeared A.D. 1135, though one of its elements, the flying buttress, had earlier been incorporated in walls or hidden under roofs, and another, the diagonal ribs at the intersections of groined cross-vaults, seems to have been first used at Durham, England about A.D. 1100. The first Gothic structure in England was erected in A.D. 1150 and in Germany in A.D. 1235. The English and, to a greater extent, the German masons modified the style to suit their own ideals. Gothic was almost wholly a Western European vogue, scarcely a genuine example of it appearing in Italy. Virtually all of the ecclesiastical, and most of the public buildings of Western Europe, for about 400 years following the middle of the 12th century, were Gothic, and its preeminence may be judged from the fact that, at the onset of the Lutheran Reformation, there were in England alone 20 cathedrals, 9000 parish churches, 645 monasteries, 90 colleges, 2374 chantries, and 110 hospitals, a total of over 12,000 structures in The Gothic.

With the advent of the Italian Renaissance and the depressing effect of the Lutheran Reformation (1517) and the English Reformation (1535), Gothic construction ceased as suddenly as it had begun, the style remaining only to be copied by succeeding generations along with the Roman, Greek, Egyptian, or other types.

The consequences were much the same in all countries; the Steinmetzen of Germany, the Compagnonnage of France, and the Freemasons of Britain lost their peculiar preeminence and were brought into competition with masons of lower grade for whom they previously had had little respect. The earliest documents portraying the brotherhoods of builders, the Regius and the Cooke MSS. of the Freemasons and the Ordinances of the Steinmetzen, come from the period of culmination of Gothic art, though the French masons, probably the most proficient in pure Gothic, left very little trace of their fraternal establishments, most of our information about them coming from a book published by Agricol Perdiguier in 1841.

Who were the actual designers of the Gothic cathedrals? Church dignitaries, Master Masons, and travelling bodies of architects have all had support, but the last named may be rejected at once as a purely imaginary explanation, without sustaining evidence. In the times of which we speak, the name, architect, was unknown, though possibly approximated by the term, ingenator. The first architects known by that name seem to have been Inigo Jones and Sir Christopher Wren in the 17th century. The Rev. James Gallaway, in *Discourses upon Architecture in England,* (1833), concluded that credit for having designed churches and cathedrals was frequently conferred upon ecclesiastics, because the only historians of the times were monks, and that churchmen probably were not so well versed in geometrical science as were Master Masons, since mathematics formed but small part of monastic learning. In "Notes on the Superintendents of English Buildings of the Middle Ages," II by Wyatt Papworth (1887), reviewed by W. H. White in *Journal of Proceedings* R. I. B. A., Vol. IV (1887),

the propositions are advanced that the Master
Masons were the designers of the Gothic edi-
fices; that neither the supposed brotherhood of
Bridge-builders, travelling from place to place,
nor the supposed bodies of travelling masons
existed; that William Wykeham was not the
designer of the building attributed to him; and
that the Abbey of Cluny was not the source of
such art. (See *History of Freemasonry* (1885)
by R. F. Gould, Ch. VI on Mediaeval Operative
Masonry; *Concise History of Freemasonry*
(1904) by the same author; and *Introduction to
Freemasonry* (1937) by Knoop and Jones). In
many instances, Master Masons rose from the
ranks. Richard Beke, who worked on London
Bridge as a mason from 1409 to 1435, became,
in the latter year, Master Mason at Canterbury
Cathedral; Henry Jenyns, aid apprentice at
Eaton College in 1453-54, was Master Mason
at St. George's Chapel, Windsor, in 1476; Thomas Teneham, an apprentice at Canterbury in
1429, and a mason there in 1433-37, and at
Eaton in 1442, was Warden at Eaton in 1448;
Christopher Horner, an apprentice at York Minster about 1480 and a mason there in 1495, was
Master Mason at York from 1505 to 1522. Some
20 other Masters of the 13th and 14th centuries are known by name, Henry Yevele being one

ARMS GRANTED TO THE CARPENTERS COMPANY,
OF LONDON, 6TH EDWARD IV, 1466.

ARMS GRANTED TO THE MASONS COMPANY,
OF LONDON, 12TH EDWARD IV, 1472-3.

ARMS OF THE SCULPTURES OR MARBLERS.
FROM THE GATESHEAD CHARTER, 1671.

ARMS OF THE FREEMASONS.
FROM THE GATESHEAD CHARTER, 1671.

ARMS OF FREEMASONS, MASONS, CARPENTERS, Etc.

Copied from the Originals and Highest Authorities.

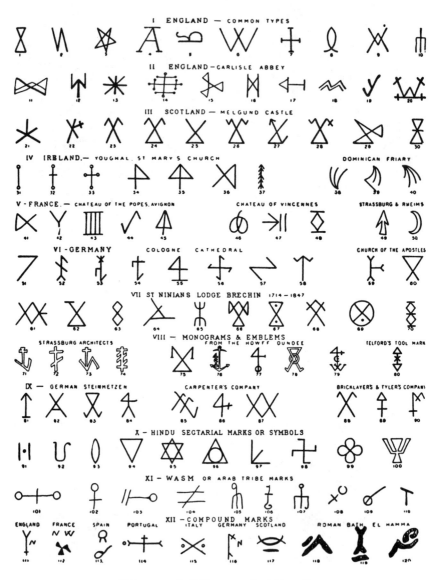

I ENGLAND — COMMON TYPES

II ENGLAND—CARLISLE ABBEY

III SCOTLAND — MELGUND CASTLE

IV IRELAND.— YOUGHAL ST MARY'S CHURCH

DOMINICAN FRIARY

V - FRANCE.— CHATEAU OF THE POPES, AVIGNON

CHATEAU OF VINCENNES

STRASSBURG & RHEIMS

VI - GERMANY   COLOGNE CATHEDRAL

CHURCH OF THE APOSTLES

VII ST NINIANS LODGE BRECHIN 1714 — 1847

VIII — MONOGRAMS & EMBLEMS
FROM THE HOWFF DUNDEE

STRASSBURG ARCHITECTS

TELFORD'S TOOL MARK

IX — GERMAN STEINMETZEN

CARPENTER'S COMPANY

BRICKLAYERS & TYLER'S COMPANY

X — HINDU SECTARIAL MARKS OR SYMBOLS

XI — WASM OR ARAB TRIBE MARKS

XII — COMPOUND MARKS
ENGLAND FRANCE SPAIN PORTUGAL ITALY GERMANY SCOTLAND   ROMAN BATH EL HAMMA

Plate of Masons' Marks.

COPIED FROM THE ORIGINALS ON THE BUILDINGS.

of the most noted and eventually becoming King's Master Mason in 1360.

Free-Masons

Quite as much disputed as the origin of the Fraternity, itself, is the derivation of the name, free-mason or freemason. In A.D. 1077, a stonemason was called "caementarius" (from caementum, small stone); in 1212, "sculptores lapidum liberorum" (sculptors of free stone) appeared; in 1217, "maszun," and, in 1300, "magister cementarius" (master mason) were used. Other terms found about the same period were "masoune," "marmorius," "lathomus," "latomos," and "lathomus." According to an old French writing, a "masoune" was to erect a house "de pere fraunche" (of free stone). In 1350, the Statute of Laborers referred to a "mestre mason de franche pere," and, in 1360, appeared the phrase, "de fraunche pere ou de grosse pere." In 1391, at Oxford, a Master Mason was called "magister lathomus liberarum petrarum," and a writ of 1415 mentioned "liberas petras" (free stone). In 1396, the contractors at Westminster Hall were called " citiens et masons de Londres," and, in the same year, there is found "lathomos vocatos ffre maceons" and "lathomos vocatos ligiers" (masons called free masons and masons called layers).

[35]

The term, freemason, was used as early as 1374 but not in connection with building operations. After 1396, "free mason," "free-mason," and "freemason" were used frequently and, in fact, continuously down to modern times. In the Statute of Laborers of 1444-5, "frank mason" was used but became "free mason" in the Statute of 1495. "Freemason" and "freemason" began to appear in general literature about 1526-1550. The old MSS. Legends and Charges usually employed the term, "mason," but the minutes of the Masons Company of London from 1620 to 1653 contain "ffremason." Crown charters used the word, "freemason" in 1604 and "ffree mason" in 1671, the latter delegating the right to make "Freemen and brethren." From about the middle of the 17th century, "mason," "free-mason," and "freemason" were used interchangeably. In 1723, the Grand Lodge of England wrote it "Free-Mason." In Scotland, the usual form was "free man" or "free man mason," but the minutes of Lodge of Edinburgh for 1636 and the Melrose copy of the *Old Charges* use the term, "frie mason."

The three principal theories advanced for the derivation of the word are (1) that it was a contraction of "free stone mason," and this is supported, especially in England, by analogy with the terms, "master mason of free stone," "sculptors of free stone," and "masons called free masons and masons called layers," used apparently to distinguish them from "hard stone hewers," a term likewise contracted to "hard hewers," and also from rough masons, wallers, layers, and setters; (2) that free-masons were those who had become free of the masons' guilds or, as itinerants, claimed exemption from guild regulation in the towns where they temporarily worked. Such seems particularly possible in Scotland where the term, "free-man mason" was used but it is claimed to be applicable to England, because we there find free carpenters, free sewers, free vintners, free dredgers, free fisherman, free linen weavers, and free gardners. But Knoop and Jones in *Introduction to Freemasonry* (1937) have pointed out that, except in London, there were no masons' guilds in England, guilds being confined to the cities, whereas the masons' trade was exercised largely in the country and required them to travel from place to place so as scarcely to permit of guild membership. This is supported by the example of the travelling minstrels, who, similarly, were without guild organization. It is also to be observed that lodges made free-masons, though they had no authority to exempt one from guild control; and (3) that, as proposed by G. F. Fort, the term, *"frere macon"* or brother mason, became corrupted into "free mason," a theory with but few adherents. Considering the breadth of meaning in the word, free, it is possible that both the first two theories are correct and that the name was differently derived in different places.

Not a great deal is known of the customs of the operative freemasons of the 16th and earlier centuries, except so far as they may be surmised from the Old Charges and from analogy with the trade guilds in other vocations. They recognized a community of interest in their mystery, which they kept to themselves; they insisted upon honest workmanship and a fair degree of morality; and they aided each other by instruction and the extension of hospitality to the traveller. The art had to be learned by precept and example and transmitted orally, for books upon such subjects hardly existed. The general illiteracy of the age was, however, of advantage to the freemasons by enabling them to control or even to monopolize the secrets of their art and to select those to whom it was thought proper to communicate it. Cowans were, presumably, those who exceeded in skill rough reasons, wallers, and setters but who, for one reason or another, were deemed unworthy to enter the Fraternity, though they were sometimes employed to work with freemasons.

Lodge

The term, lodge, has come into such general use that the incongruity of calling the meeting place of a fraternal society a sleeping place or living quarters is accepted without question. The additional meaning is of purely Masonic origin and due to the fact that the usual meeting place for operative masons was in their common lodge or lodging close by the fabric under construction. The word is so used from the earliest of the Gothic Constitutions, and the lodge has continued for five or six centuries to be the center of Masonic activity and interest. Since freemasons were accustomed to travel, the common "loge," *"logge,"* "luge" or "lodge" was the only home some of them knew. All of the Old Charges contained some such injunction as that in the Cooke MS. of the early 15th century as follows: "He shall hele (guard) the counsel of his fellows in lodge and in chamber and wherever masons meet." References to the "loge" are found in the building accounts of Vale Royal Abbey (1278), in the records of Westminster (1320), those of Carnarvon Castle (1321), and in the fabric rolls of York Minster (1355).

The curious name, tiler or tyler, applied to the outer guard and usually the custodian of the lodge is unknown, but apparently did not originate in mediaeval times, for it does not appear in print until 1735. It has been suggested that, since a tiler covered a building, so the officer who guarded or covered a secret meeting was naturally called a tiler; also that the name arose from the fact, if it is a fact, that the guard was sometimes stationed on the roof of the lodge; but, more recently, it has been traced to the French name for a stonecutter, *le tailleur de pierre,* which is no more persuasive than the other theories.

Gothic Constitutions

The oldest and most curious records of the Free-Masons are the old manuscript Legends and Charges. The Legends purport to trace the history of Masonry or Geometry from before the Flood, and the Charges contain the laws and regulations of the Craft. To these, Dr. Anderson in his *Constitutions* of 1738 first applied the name, Gothic Constitutions. In the first edition of that book (1723), only passing reference had been made to a connection of the Free-Masons with Gothic architecture, but it appears from the reconstructed minutes of Grand Lodge, first supplied in the edition of 1738, that Grand Master George Payne, in 1718, requested the brethren to bring in any old writings and records concerning Masons and Masonry, and that "several old

Copies of the Gothic Constitutions were produced and collated." This indicates that the association of Free-Masons with the Gothic had become recognized by the latter year. Only a few copies of these MSS. were available to the Grand Lodge in 1723, and probably but few more in 1738, but subsequent years have discovered a remarkable number of them, which in 1935 amounted to 99 specimens. The earlier MSS. are handwritten; some in book form and some in parchment rolls 5 to 6 inches wide and often 7 to 9 feet in length. The typical form opens with a Trinitarian Christian invocation, though this is not true of the Cooke MS. That in the Grand Lodge MS., dated A.D. 1583, reads as follows:

> "The mighte of the ffather of heaven and the wysedome of the glorious sonne through the grace and goodness of the holly ghoste yt been three p'sons and one God be with us at or beginning and give us grace so to gou'ne us here in or lyving that wee maye come to his blisse that nevr shall have ending- Amen."

The Legends begin with a reference to the seven liberal sciences, Grammar, Rhetoric, Dialectic, Arithmetic, Geometry, Music, and Astronomy, of which, Geometry was said to be the most important, because all things were measured by it. Its origin and transmission into England was then traced somewhat as follows: Lamech, who lived before the Flood, had three sons, Jabell,

Juball, and Tubal-Cain, and a daughter, Naamah. These four founded all the crafts: Jabell, Geometry; Juball, Music; Tuball-Cain, smithing; and Naamah, weaving. In preparation for the destruction of the world, they wrote these sciences upon two pillars, one of which would not burn in fire and the other of which would not drown in water. After the Flood, Hermes found one of them. Masons were present at the Tower of Babylon, the king being a Mason, loving the Craft well, and giving them Charges. Abraham and Sarah taught the sciences to the Egyptians, and Euclid, by disseminating knowledge of Geometry among the young and idle, enabled the populations to build houses and prosper. King David began the Temple at Jerusalem, which was finished by his son, Solomon, who paid the Masons well, gave them Charges and gathered them from divers countries. King Hiram (Iram or Khyrom in the various MSS.) had a son called Aynom (Aymon, Amon, Aynone, Anon, Ajuon, Benaim, or Dyan in the various MSS.), who was master of Geometry and chief Master Mason. Naymus Grecus (Namas Grecious, Naymus Graecus, Memon Grecus, or Damus Greecinus, etc., in the various MSS.) carried the science into France where Charles Martel loved Masons and gave them Charges. England was devoid of Masonry until the time of St. Albans, who walled the town of St. Albans and conferred a charter upon Masons to hold a General Assembly and gave them Charges. Divers wars destroyed Masonry until the time of King Athelstan (A.D. 920-940), whose son, Edwin (probably confused with Edwin of Northumberland of the 7th century A.D.) also loved Masons, being a master of the speculative science, and procured a charter for Masons to hold a General Assembly once a year (some MSS. say at York).

These legends are briefly and crudely stated, are entirely fanciful, abound in anachronisms, and refer for their authority to the Bible and to the polychronicons of the times. The story has a timing earlier than the legends of the German masons, which did not go back of the reign of Diocletian in the 3rd century A.D., and even earlier than the French legends which went back to Solomon's Temple. As for Charles Martel, though he is omitted from some of the MSS., there is an interesting conformity between the English and the French legends, the latter asserting that he had perpetually exempted masons from watch duty. Though there have been advanced several theories respecting the outgrowth of Masonry from the Roman Collegia, the Comacine Masters, or travelling bands of Italian architects, it is significant that the Gothic Legends do not mention Italy in the line of transmission from the East, through France, to England. The emphasis placed on the grant of charges by the various monarchs to and including Athelstan indicates a purpose to claim royal sanction for the Craft's self-government and freedom from guild or burgh control.

The manner of taking the oath by laying hands on a book is specified, after which come the Charges. These appear in different numbers and arrangements in the several MSS., some having 15 Articles for the Master and 15 Points for the Craftsmen; others, 9 for each class; still others, 9 General and 18 Special Charges for Masters and Craftsmen alike; a few, 36 General and Special charges; and some showing other variations. The substance of all, however, is much the same, the most usual provisions being the following: that they should be true men of God and Holy Church; true to the king and free from treason; true to each other; that they keep each other's counsel in lodge and in chamber; be no thieves; call each other no foul names; take no fellow's wife in villainy; that they pay truly for meat and drink; and do no villainy that might bring the Craft to shame. Masters and Craftsmen were to take no work unless they were able to finish it; to take work reasonably so that the lord or owner is well served; and to render honest work for their pay. Masters were enjoined to live honestly; pay

their fellows truly; and refrain from sup-
planting other Masters in their work. No Master or fellow was to take an apprentice for less
than seven years, or one who was not of good
birth, free born, and whole of limbs as a man
ought to be. No Mason should slander another
behind his back, or answer him ungodly; or be
a player at hazzard or dice or other unlawful
games whereby the Craft might be put to shame;
or use any leachery or be a baude, or go into the
town at night, except to a lodge or in company
with a fellow to bear witness that he was in an
honest place. Every Master and fellow was to
attend the Assembly if within 50 miles (some
say 40, 10, 7, or 5 miles) and there stand to the
award of his Masters and fellows for any tres-
passes; and not to go to the common law if possible to avoid it. Finally, every Mason was to
receive and cherish strange fellows coming over
the country and give them work, if any available, or else refresh them to the next lodge. The
MSS. all close with an exhortation similar to
that in the Grand Lodge MS. as follows:

"These Charges that we have now rehearsed unto yu all,
and all others that belong to Masons, ye shall keepe, so healpe
You God, and your hallydome, and by this book in yor hande
unto yr power, Amen, So be it."

About A.D. 1670, certain "New Articles" appeared in various MSS., of which "Harleian"

MS. No. 1942 is an example. These required that a lodge consists of at least five Freemasons, and that a sojourning brother brings with him a certificate of the time and place of his *accepcon* and have his name enrolled on a parchment. At a later date, Charges for the Apprentice appeared. All these additions reflected the changing character of the Fraternity by reason of the gradual accretion of "accepted" Masons and the insufficiency of operative regulations.

Among the more curious features of the Gothic Constitutions are the numerous textual variations and divergences in form, arrangement, language, and spelling in the face of an apparent identity in purpose, spirit, and substance. Some include, while others omit, reference to Peter Gower (Pythagoras) and the same is true of Charles Martel. Though some were obviously direct copies of others, with only clerical errors, there are many, which differ so widely as to negative this possibility. According to their conformities and divergences, the MSS. have been classified by Dr. W. Begemann and others into some four families and about twelve branches. Many of the MSS. bear dates, while the ages of others must be estimated by paleographers, it appearing therefrom that two of them are of the 15th century or earlier, one of the

16th, forty-six of the 17th, forty-five of the 18th, and five of the 19th.

The oldest, the "Regius" or "Halliwell" MS. (Brit. Mus. Reg. 17 A, i), estimated as of about 1390, is not a true Constitution and is not wholly Masonic, but appears rather to be the work of a priest-poet who was impressed by the moral precepts of the Freemasons, along with other things included in his rude verse. The MS. is written in 794 lines, expressing in rhyme the Legends and Charges of one of the Gothic Constitutions which the author had before him, to which were added the following non-Masonic items: an ordinance relating to assemblies; the legend of the Four Crowned Martyrs (Quatuor Coronati), which was a legend of the German Steinmetzen, but not of the British Freemasons; rules for behavior in church; and rules of deportment and etiquette. Such obscuration of its Masonic qualities resulted in its being listed by David Casley in his *Catalogue of the King's Library* (1734) as a "Poem of Moral Duties" and its Masonic implications went undiscovered until 1839 when Mr. Halliwell-Phillips, a non Mason, published it, calling attention to its Masonic character, which is illustrated by the following excerpts:

> "The clerk euclyde on thys wyse hytfonde
> Thys craft of gemetry yn egypte londe
> Yn egypte he tawghte hyt ful wyde

Yn duyers londe on euery syde
Mony erys aftrwarde y understonde
Yer thyt the crafte come ynto thys londe
Thys craft com ynto englond as y now say
Yn tyme of good Kyng Adelstonds day
He made tho bothe halle and eke bowre
And hye templees of gret honowre."

* * * *

"He sente aboute ynto the londe
Aftr alle the masons of the crafte
To come to hym ful euene stragfte
For to amende these defautys alle
By good consel yef hyt mytght falle
A semble thenne he cowthe let make."

The following is a portion of the fifteen Articles for the Master and the fifteen Points for the Craftsmen:

"He must love wel God, and holy Church algate
And hys mayster also, that he ys wythe."

* * * *

"The thrydde poynt must be severle
With the prentes know hyt wele,
Hys mayster cownsel he kepe and close,
And hys felows by hys goode purpose;
The prevetyse of the chamber tell he no mon,
Ny yn the logge whatsever they done,
Whatsever thou heryst, or syste him do,
Tell hyt no mon, whersever thou go."

The next oldest MS., the "Matthew Cooke" (Brit.Mus.Ad.MS.23, 198), named after him who published it in 1861, is deemed by paleographers to date from the early 15th century. It is unique in that it is clearly a copy of two earlier MSS., which, though similar, were not identical; in other words, it contains a long and a short statement of the Legends. It sets forth 9 Charges for the Master and 9 for the Craftsmen, quotes from the *Polychronicon,* and cites portions of the Old Testament as authority for some of its statements. The "William Watson" MS. of 1687, discovered in 1890, is evidently a copy. The third oldest MS. is the "Grand Lodge MS.," dated 1583, portions of which have been quoted above.

The General Assemblies referred to in all the old Constitutions pose one of the unsolved problems of medieval Masonry. How could there have been a national assembly if the Masters and Fellows were required to attend only if it were held within 50 miles (some say less) and when conditions of travel were so forbidding? Gould, *(Concise History of Freemasonry,* ch. III) argues that the General Assembly was nothing more than the annual Frankpledge, Sheriff's Turn, Shire Court, or Court Leet, held in each shire, where all crafts were required to renew their pledges of allegiance. On the other hand, the statute 3 Henry VI ch. 1, enacted in 1425, Provided:

"Whereas by the yearly congregations and confederacies, made by the Masons in their general Chapiters assembled, the good course and effect of the statutes of Laborers be openly violated and broken, in subversion of the law, and to the great damage of all the Commons; and said Lord the King willing in this case to provide a Remedy, by the advice and consent aforesaid, and at the special Request of the said Commons, hath ordained and established that such Chapiters and Congregations shall not hereafter be holden;" etc.

The possibility of general, national assemblies may be rejected on wholly practical grounds, but assemblies of more limited territorial extent may be accepted, especially as something of the kind certainly was known in Scotland.

The principal MS. Constitutions have been reproduced in facsimile in several volumes of *Quatuor Coronatorum Antigrapha,* issued by Lodge No. 2076 of London, and many particulars respecting them may be found in W. J. Hughan's *Old Charges of the British Freemasons* (1872, 1895, 1906) and in Poole and Worts' *The 'Yorkshire' Old Charges of Masons* (1935), the latter stating that, of the 99 specimens now extant, nearly 40 were produced in the North of England, 11 in Scotland, 2 in Wales, and about 5 in the Midlands, while no more than 5 can certainly be ascribed to the South of England, including London. The Legends stamp the Constitutions as of English origin, though they were to some extent current in Scotland where several copies were found in the lodges. Though none of these documents says so, it was probably deemed necessary for each fixed or permanent lodge to possess one, and there can be little doubt that both the Legends and the Charges were read to the entrant at his reception into the Fraternity, the oath being administered as therein stated. In 1670, Lodge of Aberdeen, Scotland, ordered that the Charge was to be "read at ye entering of everie entered prenteise." Alnwick Lodge in the North of England prescribed: "Noe Mason shall take any apprentice (but he must) Enter him and give him his Charge, within one whole year after." The Lodge at Swalwell, England, (now Gateshead) maintained that practice until 1754, nearly twenty years after it had affiliated with the Grand Lodge of England.

CHAPTER IV

Transition from Operative
to Speculative Masonry

HE LODGE, originally peculiar to Freemasonry, has always been the center of Masonic activity and interest, so that an
understanding of Freemasonry at any period requires a knowledge of the character and conduct of the lodges during that period. While
lodges have remained basically the same
throughout, they have varied in particulars from
time to time and from place to place; differences
and sometimes marked differences are noted
between those in England and those in Scotland; so that generalization must be indulged
only with great caution.

At the outset, something must be said about
Masons' guilds, a subject which has furnished

the material for many scholarly dissertations in endeavors to identify Freemasonry with guild organizations. These have contained much error, which has consisted in the main of two misconceptions; first, the failure to observe the almost entire absence of guilds among the British Freemasons, and, secondly, the failure to appreciate that the trade incorporations in Scotland were composed of several classes of artisans and were not Masonic. To these are added the fact that trade guilds varied so greatly in different countries and at different times that it is virtually impossible to draw generalizations respecting them over broad areas during several centuries. The incorporations, which existed in Scotland but not in England, did have considerable effect upon the operative lodges, though they included other trades, particularly the wrights (carpenters). Thus, in 1475, the municipal authorities of Edinburgh, by seal of cause, established the incorporation of Masons and wrights, and, by 1520, it had become common for the larger burghs in Scotland to grant such charters to bodies of craftsmen, allowing them certain privileges but subjecting them to municipal regulation, for example, requiring examination and approval by the Town Council for one to become a freeman of a craft or to rank as master of his trade. But such incorporations, being composed of several building trades, were distinct from the lodges of Free-Masons.

Moreover, the Masons' Craft in Scotland was governed by the Schaw Statutes of 1598 (general) and 1599 (relating particularly to Kilwinning), issued by William Schaw, Master of Work to the King from 1585. (Lawrie, *History of Freemasonry*, 1859; Lyon, *History of the Lodge of Edinburgh*, 1873; Hughan, *Masonic Sketches and Reprints*, 1871). Those statutes performed essentially the same function as the *Old Charges* in England, many injunctions in the two being substantially identical, though the statutes were accompanied by no legends, were more in the nature of formal ordinances with royal sanction, and carried very practical and persuasive penalties. A number of Scots lodges, possibly from about the middle of the 17th century, possessed copies of the English Gothic Constitutions. For the latest and most scholarly and realistic investigation of the similarities and differences between English and Scots lodges, we are indebted to Knoop and Jones *(Introduction to Freemasonry*, Manchester, 1937; *Genesis of Freemasonry*, 1947), who have pointed out that guild organizations were instrumentalities of the burghs for administration and enforcement of purely municipal regulations; that the Free-Masons performed their work principally outside the cities, moving from place to place as one work was finished and another begun; that guild organization was unsuited to their activities; and that, not only are no records preserved of masons' guilds, but, in numerous records respecting guilds, the masons were conspicuously absent.

To this, there was one exception, the Masons Company of London or, as it was chartered, "Company of ffree Masons," founded in 1376 as a true city guild. In 1472-3 it received a grant of arms from Edward IV under the name "Hole Crafte and Fellowship of Masons," the arms consisting of a black shield with an engrailled chevron on which the compasses lay extended, with three triple-towered castles of silver, two above and one below the chevron, and the motto, "The Lord is All our Trust." This grant was confirmed by Henry VIII in 1520-1, and the Company was reincorporated by Charles II in 1677. From an old account book, it appears that, prior to 1620, certain members of the Company who met in Masons' Hall were known as the "accepcon," that is, accepted Masons, and apparently constituted a lodge separate from the Company, though the latter had control of the funds of the former. This was the lodge, which, as will be noted later, summoned Elias Ashmole to attend one of its meetings in 1682. So far from being governed by guild regulations, the lodges of Freemasons afford evidence that the Craft was exempt from that control.

Nothing is known about the internal working of the lodges of the Gothic era, that is, before the middle of the 16th century. Each lodge seems to have been virtually a family of stonemasons, architects, engineers, and artists, working and dwelling together under the paternalistic despotism of the Master and his Warden. Some workmen may have spent their lives in a single lodge, that is, on a single work, since many structures required a century or more for their completion, though the disposition of the fellows to travel would lead us to infer that permanent residents were few. The Craft was a unified whole, so that the traveller was at home in any lodge where he gained employment, which he did probably by demonstrating his skill and good character. Upon the completion of an edifice, the lodge either dissolved or accompanied the Master to his new engagement.

The cement which held the Fraternity together was the common possession of the Gothic Constitutions in England, the Schaw Statutes in Scotland, the trade secrets, and the mutual assistance and benevolence which seem to have been inculcated from the very first. When the Gothic passed out of vogue, the peculiar secrets of the Craft lost much of their value, and Free-

Masons were reduced to meaner work, coming more into competition with cowans, rough masons, wallers, layers, and setters. In 17th century Scotland we find lodges dealing with small trade disputes and matters far below the dignity of cathedral building. In England, the earliest lodges of which we have information had few, if any, operative functions and only a traditional connection with architecture. In the North, therefore, lodges remained nominally operative with considerable admixture of non-operative members; While, in the South, they were essentially social and fraternal in character with only a traditional or symbolical connection with the building art, except Alnwick, near the Scots border and undoubtedly influenced by Scots customs, which remained operative until its expiration in 1763.

The dates of the oldest preserved records of lodges in Scotland are as follows: Aitchison's-Haven Lodge, 1598; Lodge of Edinburgh, 1599; Glasgow St. John Lodge No. 3 (bis), 1620; Kilwinning Lodge No. 0, 1642; Scoon and Perth Lodge, 1658; Aberdeen Lodge No. 1 (ter), 1670; Melrose St. John Lodge No. 1 (bis), 1674; Canongate Kilwinning Lodge No. 2, 1677; and Lodge of Dunblane No. 9,1696. But some of the lodges are shown by extraneous records to be much older, thus, Aberdeen Lodge can be traced back to 1483; Kilwinning Lodge, to 1599; Lodge of St. John at Kelso, 1599; Ancient Lodge No. 49 of Dundee, 1600; Lodge of St. Andrew No. 52 at Banff, 1600; and Glasgow St. John's Lodge, 1613. Several of these, notably Kilwinning and Aberdeen, claim to have been founded in the 12th to the 14th centuries. It has never been satisfactorily determined which lodge is the oldest, though Edinburgh and Kilwinning have each at times headed the list prepared by the Grand Lodge of Scotland. When the former, which had once been awarded No. 1 was later subordinated to "Mother" Kilwinning, the latter was assigned No. 0 to avoid renumbering the remaining lodges, and similar shifts in precedence among other lodges have been accompanied by the additions of "bis" or "ter" to the numbers.

In England, the oldest minutes extant are those of Alnwick Lodge (1701) and York Lodge (1712), though minutes of the latter for 1705 were once reported as examined, having later disappeared. For information as to the existence and character of English lodges in the 17th century, we are forced to rely solely on extraneous references, of which there are half a dozen. These all come from men of superior attainments, that is, "gentlemen," and none from those following the stonemasons' trade. The first of these was Elias Ashmole, F. R. S., a prominent antiquary and curiosity-seeker, who later founded the Ashmolean

Museum. His diary states that he was made a Mason at Warrington in Lancashire, October 16, 1646, at 4:30 P.M., with Col. Henry Mainwaring of Karincham in Cheshire. Investigation has developed the fact that, of the seven members of the lodge then present, none was a working stonemason. There is no further trace of this lodge. Ashmole's reception has been used to support the contention that a connection existed between Freemasonry and Rosicrucianism, because, as alleged, Ashmole was an adept of the latter philosophy and was instrumental in weaving much of its doctrine into the Masonic rituals. But there is no proof that he was a Rosicrucian, although it is not improbable that, as a curiosity-seeker, he dabbled in it for much the same reason that he entered the Lodge at Warrington, that is, for information. There is no evidence that he took much interest in the Fraternity, for evidently he did not again attend lodge for thirty-five years. His diary tells us that:

"March 1682.
" 10-About 5 P. M. I rec'd: a Summons to app r at a Lodge to be held the next day, at Masons Hall London.
"11-Accordingly I went, & about Noone were admitted into the Fellowship of Freemasons,
"Sr William Knight, Capt. Rich. Borthwick, Mr. Will: Woodman, Mr. Wm. Grey, Mr. Samuell Taylour and Mr. William Wise.
"I was the Senior Fellow among them (it being 35 years

since I was admitted). There were present beside myself the Fellows after named.

"Mr. Tho: Wise, Mr. of the Masons Company this present years. Mr. Thomas Shorthose, Mr. Thomas Shadbolt, Waindsford Esqr: Mr. Nich: Young, Mr. John Shorthose, Mr. William Hamon, Mr. John Thompson, & Mr. Will: Stanton.

"We all dyned at the Halfe Moone Taverne in Cheapside, at a noble dinner prepared at the charge of the new-accepted Masons."

Ashmole died in 1692, a quarter of a century before the organization of the Grand Lodge of England and his influence is not likely to have been felt on the rituals used by that body.

Dr. Robert Plot, was unfavorably impressed by the Freemasons and devoted considerable space to them in his *Natural History of Staffordshire* (1686), saying that he found them dispersed more or less over the nation, particularly in the Moorlands; that persons of the most eminent quality did not disdain to be of that fellowship; that they had a large parchment volume containing the history and rules of the Craft; that their meeting was called a lodge, which must consist of five or six of the ancients of the Order, whom the candidate presented with gloves; that admission consisted of communicating certain secret signs whereby they were known to one another all over the nation and had maintenance wherever they traveled; and that, if a Mason gave one of these signs, his fellow was obliged to come to him even from the top of a steeple, and assist him. Plot found fault with the incoherence of the Gothic Legends, called attention to the statute of Henry VI against congregations and assemblies of Masons, and suggested that such chapters might well be looked into lest they do mischief.

John Aubrey, not a Freemason, left a MS., "Natural History of Wiltshire," written in 1656-86, in which he referred to the "Fraternity of Freemasons (adopted Masons)" who had

"Severall-Lodges in severall Counties for their reception; and when any of them fall into decay, the brotherhood is to relieve him &c. The manner of their adoption is very formall and with an oath of secrecy."

Aubrey also left a memorandum written May 18, 1691, stating that, on that day, Sir Christopher Wren, Sir Henry Goodric of the Tower, and others were to be adopted as brothers in a convention of Accepted Masons (the word "Free" had been stricken and "Accepted" substituted). It is doubted that Wren ever became a member of the Fraternity.

Randle Holme (third of the name), deputy to the Garter King of Arms, in his *Acadamie of Armory* (1688), said:

"I cannot but Honor the Fellowship of Masons because of its antiquity; and the more as being a member of that society, called Freemasons. In being conversant amongst them I have observed the use of these several Tools following some whereof I have seen born in Coats of Armour."

Among his effects, were found two scraps of paper, one of which read:

"There is seurall words & signes of a freemason to be revailed to you wch as yu will answ: before God at the Great & terrible day of Judgement yu keep secret & not revaile the same to any in the heares of any pson w but to the Mrs. & fellows of the said Society of freemasons so help me God &c."

The second was headed: "William Wade wt giue for to be a freemason," followed by twenty-six names, among which were "Ran Holme," "Willm Street Aldm.," and "Sam Pike tailer." This was apparently the list of members of the lodge at Chester where Holme lived.

A leaflet printed in London in 1698 attacked Freemasonry as being a "devilish sect of men," "anti-Christ," "Evil-doers," and "corrupt people," and warned all "godlike people in the citie of London" about the "mischiefs and Evil practices in Sight of God by those called Freed Masons," and to "take Care lest their Ceremonies and secret Swearings take hold of you; and be wary that none cause you to err from Godliness."

Jonathan Belcher, Governor of Massachusetts and New Hampshire, stated in 1741 that he had been admitted to the Society thirty-seven years previously, that is, in 1704, when he is known to have been in England.

That the Society was well known to the London public is indicated by two references made by Richard Steele (later Sir) in the *Tatler* in 1709 and 1710 where, discussing a coterie of London dandies, he said: "They have their signs and tokens like Freemasons," and "they have secret Intimations of each other like the Freemasons."

A pamphlet was published in London in 1710 by A. Baldwin, consisting of *A Letter from a Clergy-man of London,* which referred to "the Word, Mark, or Token of a certain Company called the Free Masons, which is well known to every Member of that Sage Society, but kept a mighty Secret from all the World besides."

Our earliest acquaintance with Freemasonry in Ireland discloses the non-operative character of the lodges and also their mixed composition. At the University of Dublin, July 11, 1688, John Jones, A. B., afterwards D. D., delivered a tripos or screed depicting an imaginary lodge of Freemasons to be instituted in the University and to be composed of gentlemen, mechanics, porters, parsons, ragmen, hucksters, divines, tinkers, knights, thatchers, cobblers, poets, justices, drawers, beggars, aldermen, paviors, sculls, freshmen, bachelors, scavengers, masters, sawgelders, doctors, ditchers, pimps, lords, butchers, and tailors, who should bind themselves by an oath never to discover their mighty no-secret, and to relieve whatsoever strolling distressed brethren they met with, after the example of Freemasons in and about Trinity College, by whom a collection was lately made for a reduced brother. This shows that the Society was familiar to Dublin citizens in 1688 as one composed of diverse social strata, possessing secrets, and assisting distressed brethren.

The transition of the lodges from operative to speculative character differed from place to place and occupied in all above two centuries. Alnwick Lodge was operative and remained so until its demise in 1763, while York Lodge seems to have tended the other way, George Tempest, Baronet, being Master in 1705, and the Lord Mayor of the City being Master two years later. Though lodges in Scotland kept up their operative functions, at least nominally, admittance of non-operatives began as early as the year 1600, as shown by the presence of John Boswell, Laird of Aichinleck, in Lodge of Edinburgh June 6 of that year, and the acceptance of similar personages in that lodge are frequently recorded in subsequent years. For Scots lodges as a whole, there was an overlap of about two centuries between the first recorded presence of non-operative members and the last operative proceedings.

The first minute records of non-operative members in the several lodges are as follows: Lodge of Edinburgh, 1600; Lodge of St. John at Kelso, 1652; Lodge of Aberdeen, 1670; Kilwinning Lodge, 1672; Lodge of Melrose, 1675; Lodge of Dunblane, 1696; and Lodge of Glasgow, 1842; while the last references to operative matters found in the minutes are as follows: Lodge of St. Andrew, 1703; Lodge of St. John at Kelso, 1705; Lodge of Edinburgh, 1709; Kilwinning Lodge, 1725; Lodge of Aberdeen, 1781; and Lodge of Glasgow, St. John No. 3 (bis), did not accept non-operatives until about 1842 and after it had affiliated with the Grand Lodge of Scotland.

What was the reason for this metamorphosis of British Freemasonry; what attraction did early stonemasons' lodges have for other tradesmen, gentlemen, and even the nobility; why was this not paralleled in France and Germany? These questions have never been satisfactorily answered. The transition proceeded without plan and at a tempo entirely dependent on local conditions, being marked in some lodges and entirely lacking in others until comparatively late dates. Though, in Scotland, theoretic activities long remained rarely appendant to operative functions, in England, operative Masonry became only traditional or symbolical. It is not strange that Dr. Plot remarked in 1686 the admission of the nobility or that John Jones at Dublin in 1688 made sport of the admixture of social classes; but it is strange that this commingling occurred in spite of the social stratification which the British people have so long insisted upon. It is not likely that the lodges sought "accepted" Masons in order to bolster up their waning fortunes, for it is hardly possible that the entrants would have permitted themselves to be used in that way. It is more likely that lodges had always admitted some honorary members, such as church dignitaries, local squires, magistrates, and owners of the works, the "accepted" or "adopted" Masons feeling reassured by the Legends which recited the long patronage of the Craft by kings, princes, and learned men. It is not to be doubted that a squire or an earl would have counted it an honor to enjoy vicarious credit for a cathedral or other outstanding landmark of his burgh or county, which dominated the landscape and around which local legends clustered.

Regularity of meetings as indicated by minutes kept and preserved in the north was much neglected in the south, where, according to the Old Charges, any five or six Masons might form a lodge, accept candidates, and close or even permanently dissolve, though, at York, London, and possibly other places, the times and places of meeting were more definite and the occupancy

Burlesque Procession of Scald Miserables in 1741

Apple-Tree Tavern

The Goose and Gridiron Tavern at London in 1717
The Grand Lodge of England was Organized in this Building

of offices more permanent. Implicit in this loose procedure were difficulties in distinguishing duly made Masons from impostors, so that, by the close of the third quarter of the 17th century, certain "New Articles" appeared in some of the Old Charges, of which "Harleian" MS. No. 1942 is an example, requiring the sojourning Mason to carry some written identification and become enrolled in the lodge to be attended.

At the close of the 17th century, there were no less than 15 and possibly 20 lodges in Scotland, but, in England, we are assured of only the Lodges at York and Alnwick, with the possible addition of the Four Old Lodges which met to form the Grand Lodge in 1717. In the whole of the 17th century, we find traces of only five others, viz., the lodge which admitted Ashmole at Warrington in 1646; a probable lodge at Chester to which Randle Holme belonged; the lodge attended by Ashmole at Masons Hall in 1682; a lodge mentioned by John Aubrey as scheduled to meet at St. Paul's Church, May 18, 1691; and a probable lodge at Scarborough.

The dearth of English lodge records led Dr. Plot *(Natural History of Staffordshire)*, Governeur Pownall *(Archaelogia*, IX, p. 118), and Thomas Hope *(Historical Essay on Architecture*, 3rd ed., 1840) to conclude that the lodges were dissolved by the statute 3 Hen. VI and that Freemasonry was obliterated, except for traces which became idle clubs. But Gould *(History of Freemasonry,* Vol. 1, p. 350) attributes these comments to a misreading of the statute, which applied to Masons in their "generalx chapiterez assemblez" and not to general chapters and assemblies, and he asserts that not all Masonic assemblies were proscribed but only the general chapters assembled where wage agreements were made. The fact that some lodges were openly held seems to discount the idea of complete prohibition and leaves us to infer that the decadence of English lodges was the result rather of changes in economic and social conditions.

Though Gothic architecture flourished on the continent of Europe contemporaneously with that in the British Isles, continental lodges did not transform into speculative societies. When, following the formation of the Grand Lodge at London, lodges were established in Europe, they encountered nothing that resembled themselves or the Freemasonry that they practiced. The origin of Freemasonry, therefore, lay in the Scots and English lodges of Freemasons engaged in the fabrication of Gothic structures in the 14th century and probably as early as the 12th century when that style arose.

CHAPTER V

British Freemasonry in the Eighteenth Century

The Grand Lodge of England

I N 1716-17, there were at least four lodges meeting in or near London, known as the lodges which met (1) at the Goose and Gridiron Ale House in St. Paul's Churchyard; (2) at the Crown Ale House in Parker's Lane near Drury Lane; (3) at the Apple-Tree Tavern in Charles Street, Covent Garden; and (4) at the Rummer and Grapes Tavern in Channel Row Westminster. Three of these still exist; (1) became Antiquity Lodge No. 2; (2) expired in 1740; (3) became Fortitude and Old Cumberland Lodge No. 12, though its antiquity is disputed, because of a reorganization and a new charter in 1723, hence, its high number; and (4) became Royal Somerset House and Inverness Lodge No. 4. The last named was long known as the "Horn"

Lodge. We know very little about the character or composition of the Four Old Lodges in 1716-72, since the only account of their activities in those times comes from reconstructed minutes of the Grand Lodge published by Dr. James Anderson more than twenty years later in his *Constitutions of 1738.* So far as we can judge, these lodges were mixtures of gentlemen, scholars, and operative craftsmen, and were largely social in character, though retaining sufficient of the operative tradition to render appropriate the participation of carpenters, stonecutters, and blacksmiths.

We are informed by Dr. Anderson that, in 1716, these lodges and some "old Brothers" met at the Apple-Tree Tavern and, placing the oldest Master Mason in the Chair, constituted themselves a Grand Lodge pro tempore, revived the Quarterly Communication of officers of lodges, "call'd the Grand Lodge," and resolved to hold the Annual Assembly and Feast and choose a Grand Master. Accordingly, on St. John Baptist's Day, June 24, 1717, the "Assembly and Feast of the Free and Accepted Masons" was held at the Goose and Gridiron Ale House, and Mr. Anthony Sayer, Gentleman, was chosen Grand Master and Mr. Jacob Lamball, carpenter, and Capt. Joseph Elliot, Grand Wardens. The next year, George Payne, Esq. was elected Grand Master and Mr. John Cordwell, city carpenter, and Mr. Thomas Morrice, stone-cutter, Grand Wardens. The Grand Master requested the brethren to bring in any old writings or records concerning Masons or Masonry in order to show the usages of ancient times, and several old copies of the Gothic Constitutions were produced. June 24, 1719, the Reverend Brother John Theophilus Desaguliers, L.L.D., F.R.S. was elected Grand Master and Mr. Anthony Sayer and Mr. Tho. Morrice, Grand Wardens. Several old brethren who had neglected the Craft visited the lodges, and some noblemen were admitted, and more new lodges were constituted. George Payne was again elected Grand Master in 1720 and Mr. Thomas Hobby, stone-cutter, and Mr. Rich. Ware, mathematician, Grand Wardens. In this year, the first Quarterly Communications were held, one on St. John the Evangelist's Day, December 27th, 1720, and the other on Lady Day, 1721. Dr. Anderson called all such Quarterly Communications Grand Lodges, reserving the term, Annual Assembly and Feast, for the meetings on June 24 of each year. The General Regulations, which the *Constitutions of 1723* inform us were drawn by George Payne in 1720 and approved June 24, 1721, provided in Articles XII and XIII that the Grand Lodge consisted of the Masters and Wardens of lodges, the Grand Master, his Deputy, and the Grand Wardens, and was to meet about Michaelmas, Christmas, and Lady Day, and the latter Article contains the cryptic and much discussed passage: "Apprentices must be admitted Masters and Fellow-Craft only here, unless by a Dispensation." Regulation XXII explained that the Annual Communication and Feast on June 24 consisted of the brethren of all lodges in and about London and Westminster, but, elsewhere, the term Grand Lodge is used generically to include both the Quarterly and Annual Communications.

At the Assembly and Feast, June 24, 1721, 12 lodges were represented, Lord Stanhope, Earl of Chesterfield and others were made Masons, and the first nobleman to assume the office, the Duke of Montagu, was installed Grand Master, with John Beal, M. D. as his Deputy. Then followed three important Quarterly Communications, those of September 29 and December 27, 1721 and March 25, 1722, at which 16, 20, and 24 lodges, respectively, were represented. At the first, the Duke of Montagu, finding fault with all copies of the Gothic Constitutions, ordered Dr. Anderson to digest them in a new and better method, that is to say, the Old Charges were to be rephrased so as to apply more appropriately to a purely speculative society. At the next meeting, a committee of fourteen was appointed to examine Dr. Anderson's work, and, at the Meeting in March 1722, his *History, Charges, Regulations, and Master's Song* received approval of the committee and were ordered to be printed. According to Dr. Anderson, a serious schism was then narrowly avoided, though some doubt his story, supporting their challenge with arguments none too convincing. It having been proposed to continue the Duke of Montagu in office for another year, the Duke of Wharton, described as a man of somewhat changeable political principles and indifferent fortune, assembled a number of the Craft in a meeting, June 24, 1722, and had himself proclaimed Grand Master, with Mr. Joshua Timson, blacksmith, and Mr. William Hawkins, mason, Grand Wardens. But Montagu healed the breach by assembling the Grand Lodge, January 17, 1723, and having Wharton proclaimed Grand Master, with Dr. Desaguliers as Deputy and Joshua Timson and Dr. Anderson as Grand Wardens, the latter in place of Hawkins, "who was always out of town." At this meeting, Dr. Anderson's *Book of Constitutions* was approved in print, 25 lodges being represented. Dr. Anderson's minutes end with the meeting of April 25, 1723, after which the minutes were officially recorded and preserved.

The *Constitutions of 1723*, the most important document coming from the premier Grand Lodge contained a fanciful and neither credible nor creditable "history" of Masonry, being an expansion and elaboration of, but little improvement on, the Gothic Legends; six Charges of a Free-Mason, a rather faithful speculative modification of the Old Charges; the General Regulations of 1721, containing elaborate provisions for the government of Masons, lodges and Grand Lodges; a group of songs; and the approbation of the Grand Officers and the officers of some twenty lodges.

The events of 1717-1723, often called the "Revival," have been the subject of much comment and many differences of opinion, and Dr. Anderson has been the object of considerable criticism, often severe. While he was imaginative and unreliable as a historian, he probably was not guilty of such duplicity or deceit as that charged by such writers as Lionel Vibert, whose criticism itself does-not bear logical analysis throughout. The times and the pioneering nature of Dr. Anderson's work must be considered.

As represented by the *Constitutions of 1723* and also those of 1738, the movement of 1717-23 was, for many years, regarded as the revival of a Grand Lodge and of Quarterly Communications which had fallen into decay through the neglect of the putative Grand Master, Sir Christopher Wren, the celebrated architect of St. Paul's Cathedral, who, however, was probably not even a member of the Society. If the fact were otherwise, it is strange that nothing seems to have been known of it in 1723, for the *Constitutions* of that year attribute to him no such position. It was not alone to Dr. Anderson but also to the disinclination of Masonic writers for a century and a half to make any investigations for themselves that the idea so long persisted that Freemasonry, including the Three Degrees, was of very ancient origin, dating back at least to the time of King Solomon's Temple and possibly further.

The changes wrought by the new organization may be generalized as follows: (1) A Grand Lodge was formed to unify Masonry and regulate lodges in London and Westminster; (2) Stated Annual and Quarterly Communications were prescribed, in the former of which the general membership enjoyed a limited participation, and the latter of which included only Grand Officers and the Masters and Wardens of lodges; (3) Authority to form or warrant new lodges was vested in the Grand Master; (4) The Old Charges were rephrased in speculative form and thirty-nine new General Regulations were adopted; (5) All pretense at the administration of operative matters was abandoned, and stonemasons, as such, ceased to have any particular claim on the Society; (6) The Grand Mastership came to be considered as appropriately held only by a nobleman and Grand Wardenships were no longer conferred on tradesmen or operatives; (7) Degrees were formulated, legends supplemented, and rituals elaborated; and (8) Nominal adherence to Christianity was abandoned and a nonsectarian natural religion adopted.

There was neither a revival, a revolution, nor a creation, yet elements of each were present. On the stem of operative customs, laws, and forms there was grafted the symbolism, rituals, and moral science of a new system, called symbolic or speculative Masonry; the Old Charges, Legends, and usages were worked over, codified and reformed, but the basic tenets and customs of the prior system were adhered to. The new structure was built upon the foundation of the old; the practical art was spiritualized into a theoretic moral science, illustrated by symbolism drawn from architecture; and the laws and customs of the stonemasons' trade were applied to social, moral, and fraternal purposes. Mackey said: "The ship was still there but the object of the voyage was changed."

British Freemasonry 1723-1750

Freemasonry immediately sprang into prominence and, though increasing in numbers of both lodges and members, became the object of imitation and denunciation. Although, at first, claiming jurisdiction only in London and Westminster, the Grand Lodge, eventually and by implied consent, came to have authority throughout England, except at York and Alnwick where independent lodges existed. Rival societies sprang up, some friendly, though dissident, and some openly scornful of the new body. In the first class must be placed the St. John Masons, who were not an organization but consisted of those who had belonged to the old Christian lodges and who had not affiliated with the new regime, though records show that they visited the new lodges repeatedly and were recognized as legitimate Masons. Among them, there probably was an element unreconciled to the changes, for Dr. Anderson tells us that, in 1720, valuable manuscripts were burned lest they fall into strange hands. The Lodges at York and Alnwick remained aloof, the former purporting, in 1725, to organize itself into the "Grand Lodge of All England."

Of the imitative bodies, which were more or less Masonic, little is known, our information coming mostly from occasional newspaper notices or comments. The following are heard of in the years respectively given as follows: (1) Philo-Musicae et Architecturae Societas Apolloni,

(1725-27); (2) Apollonian Masons, (1726), possibly the same as (1); (3) Antediluvian Masons, (1726); (4) Real Masons, (1726-31); (5) Honorary Masons, (1730-39); (6) Modern Masons, (1741-74); and (7) Scald Miserable Masons, (1742).

The three following were not Masonic at all but considered themselves rivals of Masonry. (A) Noble Order of Bucks, (1722-73); (B) Ancient Noble Order of Gormogons, (1724-31); and (C) Order of Gregorians, (1730-97).

Adding to the annoyance of the Grand Lodge was a flood of pamphlets pretending to expose the ritual and secrets of Freemasonry and also intended to bring ridicule upon it, as above enumerated in Chapter II.

During this period, Freemasonry expanded vertically and horizontally—vertically by the addition of degrees and horizontally by migrating over most of the civilized globe. The example set by the formation of a Grand Lodge at London was followed in Ireland in 1730 and in Scotland in 1736, and the growth of Freemasonry may be judged somewhat by the fact that, in the latter year, there were approximately 100 lodges in Scotland, 33 of which participated in forming the Grand Lodge and were soon joined by all the others.

The first entrance of British Freemasonry

into foreign lands cannot be ascertained clearly from the records. It is asserted that a lodge met in Belgium as early as 1721 and one at Paris in 1725, both unchartered, although the latter was definitely warranted sometime before 1732. The first lodge warranted in a foreign land of which there is express record was one formed by the Grand Master, the Duke of Wharton, in person at Madrid, Spain, in 1728. The next was warranted for Bengal, India, in 1730. An unwarranted lodge began meeting at Philadelphia, Pa., as early as 1730, but the first chartered lodge in America was old First Lodge at Boston, Mass., in 1733. Then followed lodges at Hamburg, Germany, 1733; Savannah, Ga., 1734; Holland, 1734; Rome, Italy, 1735; Sweden, 1735; Portugal, 1735-6; Charleston, S. C., 1736; Portsmouth, N. H., 1736; Switzerland, 1736; West Indies, 1737; Dresden, Germany, 1738; Nova Scotia, 1738; New York, 1739; Poland, 1739; Turkey, 1738 or 48; Berlin, Germany, 1740; Russia, 1740; Bayreuth, Germany, 1741; Virginia, 1741; Austria, 1742; Frankfurt, Germany, 1743; Denmark, 1743; Newfoundland, 1746; Newport, R. I., 1749; Maryland, 1749; and New Haven, Conn., 1750.

Thus, in the short space of 33 years, Freemasonry had entered virtually all of the countries of the northern hemisphere, making probably the most rapid expansion ever exhibited by a society, a doctrine, or a philosophy, notwithstanding it met some misgivings on the part of monarchs and encountered the enmity of the Church of Rome, beginning with the Bull, *In Eminenti*, promulgated by Pope Clement XII, April 28, 1738. By mid century there were several Provincial Grand Lodges in Europe, in addition to the one warranted at Boston, Mass., in 1733, and more or less independent Grand Lodges seem to have been formed in France and Germany about 1740-41.

But the Grand Lodge of England paid very little attention to its lodges abroad, even those in the American Colonies, and was not even careful in keeping records of them. Provincial Grand Masters were the personal appointees of the Grand Master in Britain and held office during his pleasure, but they seldom reported to the Grand Secretary, except on the formation of a new lodge and then only to secure the necessary charter. The noble Grand Masters usually left the details of administration to their Deputies.

By 1738, the machinery of the Grand Lodge had begun to deteriorate and, during the reign of Lord Byron, the last Grand Master of this period, who grievously neglected the Craft, affairs were in a far from satisfactory condition. Many lodges, even those meeting in London, were erased for failure to pay their Grand Lodge dues or for other irregularities, and, in general, it seemed that the Grand Lodge had entered upon a decline. The situation was not helped by the formation in 1751 of a rival body, the Ancient Grand Lodge, which contended for precedence during the rest of the century. Freemasonry was progressing by its own inherent virtue rather than by wise administration of the Grand Lodge.

The half century following the formation of the Grand Lodge of England is regrettably poor in Masonic literature and in sources from which one may judge the character of lodges, doctrine, ceremonies, or the general content of Freemasonry of the time. With the exception of public processions on St. John Days and other gala occasions, of which it was very fond but which were eventually much restricted, the Grand Lodge was retiring, attended strictly to its own business, and seems to have discouraged the discussion of Masonic affairs on the outside. There is also the probability, if we may judge from the Masonic books, which appeared many years later, that there was little of spiritual or stimulating character in the early doctrine to form the basis for literary discussion. Beyond the *Constitutions,* a few manuals, and such addresses as have been preserved, for examples, that of Francis Drake F.R.S. at York Lodge in 1726 and Martin *Clare's Defense of Masonry* in

1730, virtually nothing issued from the Grand Lodge or any well informed Freemason about the purposes or ideals of the Society. We learn as much from the exposes issued by enemies as we do from anything emanating from friends of the Fraternity.

Grand Lodges of Ireland and Scotland

The Grand Lodge of England is often called the Mother Grand Lodge of the World. As meaning that it is the oldest or that it originated the Grand Lodge system, this statement is correct, but if it is intended to intimate that all other Grand Lodges sprang from it or were organized by its authority, the statement is in error. There is evidence that non-operative Masonry was known in Ireland as early as 1688, and the lodges in Scotland had, even earlier, begun to admit non-operative members.

In 1725, Anderson's *Constitutions* was on sale in Dublin bookstores, and mention is made of a Grand Lodge, probably that for the Province of Munster, as early as July 17, 1725. The earliest extant minutes of an Irish lodge are those for December 8, 1726, recorded in a volume containing the minutes of both a private lodge at Cork and the Grand Lodge for the Province of Munster. The origin of the Grand Lodge of Ireland is obscure, due to the loss or destruction

THE
CONSTITUTIONS
OF THE
FREE-MASONS
CONTAINING THE
Hiſtory, Charges, Regulations, &c.
of that moſt Ancient and Right
Worſhipful *FRATERNITY*.

For the Uſe of the LODGES.

L O N D O N:

Printed by WILLIAM HUNTER, for JOHN SENEX at the *Globe,*
and JOHN HOOKE at the *Flower-de-luce* over-againſt *St. Dunſtan's*
Church, in *Fleet-ſtreet.*

In the Year of Maſonry ———— 5723
Anno Domini ———— ———— 1723

each thing

ALSO that ye should be~
Leigemen to the King of England
without Treason or any other
Falsehood and that ye know
no Treason or Treachery but
you amend privitly if ye may
or else warn the King or his
Council thereof.

ALSO ye shall be true one
to each other that is to say to
every Mason of the Craft of
Masonry that be Masons?
allowed ye shall Do unto them
as ye would they should Do
unto you

ALSO that ye shall keep~
all

refresh him with money unto
the next Lodge

And also that every Ma-
son shall truely serve the Lord
for his pay and every Master
truely to make an end of his
Work be it Task or Journey~
if he have his demand and
all that he ought to have?.

These Charges that we
have now rehearsed unto
you and all others that
belong to Masons ye
shall keep; So help you
God and your Halidome~

Amen~

Fac-simile Page from the Original M. S. of the Ancient Constitutions of Free and Accepted Masons, A. D., 1726 of records and the confusion between it and the Munster body. It seems to be agreed that Lord Kingston, who had been Grand Master of England in 1729, was elected Grand Master of Ireland at the institution of the Grand Lodge there in 1730. The following year, he was elected Grand Master of the Munster body, which, however, seems to have lapsed in 1733.

The first Irish *Book of Constitutions* was based on Anderson's *Constitutions of 1723* and was published by John Pennell in 1730, and a second edition appeared in 1751, based on Anderson's *Constitutions of 1738.* The Grand Lodge, small at first, began to prosper about 1747. In 1885 it had 387 lodges, though it had warranted 1014, and, in 1939, it had 700 lodges, of which 65 were outside of Ireland. It was very active in issuing warrants for traveling or military lodges, and, in 1813, had 122 such lodges.

Scotland was the last of the three British countries to adopt the speculative or Grand Lodge system. Just when the English ritualistic work was introduced there, we do not know, but it was probably accepted gradually by the various lodges from about 1721 and had become established in Edinburgh as early as 1729, though some lodges tenaciously adhered to their operative practices.

At the time of the organization of the Grand

Lodge, there were at least 100 lodges in Scotland. Canongate Kilwinning Lodge originated this step in 1735 when it proposed that a Grand Master for Scotland be elected. At a convention of 33 lodges, held November 30, 1736, William St. Clair of Roslin was elected Grand Master, although he had become a Master Mason only eight days before.

The Grand Lodge of Scotland and its lodges have always adhered strictly to the three degrees of Craft Masonry, but, due to some circumstance which has never been thoroughly explained, they have been credited with instituting numerous higher degrees, some of which are now included in the Scottish Rite and all of which originated on the continent. Kilwinning Lodge, on account of its primacy among Scots lodges, has been the especial object of this assertion, though it never worked any but the three degrees.

It has never been definitely determined which is the oldest lodge in Scotland, the Grand Lodge having changed the official ranking of the lodges several times. For some years now, Kilwinning Lodge has enjoyed that precedence, being numbered No. 0 when it was set ahead of Lodge of Edinburgh No. 1. Several lodges in Scotland can show by minutes and others by extraneous references that they existed many years before any known reference to an English lodge, and any one of half a dozen may be older than Kilwinning or Edinburgh. A number of lodges outside the British Isles are under Scots warrants.

The organization of the Grand Lodge at London in 1717 gave it no authority in Ireland or Scotland, and the fact is that, at first, it claimed authority in only London and Westminster. It gradually came to have jurisdiction throughout England by general acquiescence and not by any declaration of its own. While the Irish and Scots Crafts adopted generally the English forms, ceremonies, and regulations, they were each completely autonomous and each organized and operated solely under its own authority.

Degrees

One of the peculiarities of Freemasonry is its employment of degrees in its initiatory ceremonies, although the system is said to have existed in the Ancient Mysteries and has been copied by other modern fraternal orders. The question as to when and how the three degrees of Entered Apprentice, Fellow Craft, and Master Mason originated has enticed and perplexed Masonic students during the past century, and still may be regarded as unsettled. Of course, the three grades of workmen have been recognized from early times in numerous occupations, that is, the indentured apprentice, bound to a fellow or master usually for seven years to learn the trade; the fellow, fellow of craft, or journeyman (day worker), who was a finished workman and artisan; and the master, who was only an unusually able fellow of craft, having the ambition and administrative ability to undertake the direction and completion of a whole work. But the term degree, so far as relative to modern Masonic degrees, must be confined to a secret ceremony of admission or advancement, including the communication of particular, distinguishing words, signs, or other esoteric matter, those of each succeeding degree being withheld from members of a lower degree or degrees. Unless it is so limited, the discussion becomes pointless.

The great preponderance of evidence contained in the minutes of lodges in Scotland and the scant minutes and extraneous references in England indicate but a single ceremony for "admitting" or "entering" the Apprentice in the North and the "making," "admission," "acceptance," or "adoption" of a Mason in the South. Such may be called negative evidence but it is, nevertheless, quite convincing in volume. We encounter some peculiarities in Scotland in the interposition of the grade of "entered apprentice" or "enter'd 'prentice," for it seems that a mere apprentice was not a member of the lodge but became such only on his "entry" by having his name recorded in the lodge books. Also, in Scotland, there seems to have been observed some ceremony in "passing" an Entered Apprentice to a Fellow Craft, and the possibility that, at this point, separate and additional secrets were imparted furnishes the principal argument supporting the existence of a pre Grand Lodge system of two degrees. But the Schaw *Statutes* (1598-9) required a lodge for the reception of Fellow Crafts and Masters to consist of six Masters and two Entered Apprentices, so that the latter would appear to have possessed all esoteric knowledge, and, in some instances, they were elected to preside over lodges. Theoretic Masons were, sometimes admitted as Apprentices and sometimes as Fellow Crafts or Masters, but, throughout, the "Mason Word" is referred to as the ultimate esoteric matter and as possessed by all grades. By reason of the greater emphasis which, in Scotland, was placed on operative affairs, it is possible that some effort was made to distinguish between the esoteric knowledge of the several grades, yet, it is significant that the only secret mentioned is referred to in the singular, "Mason Word." It is thought that, by the later part of the 17th century, the Mason Word had come to include grips and signs as well as a word.

In England, we find no hint of any gradation in the pre Grand Lodge era. Ashmole tells us that, in 1646, he was "made a Free Mason" and that, at Masons Hall in 1682, certain men were "admitted into the Fellowship of Freemasons." At York, the lodge minutes from 1712 to 1725 uniformly use the term, "admitted and sworn." The formulation of esoteric ceremonies, with secrets appropriate to each, thus forming degrees, was probably done by the founders of the Grand Lodge. The concept of an Entered Apprentice degree and a Fellow Craft degree probably arose solely from the obvious operative distinction between the two ranks, rather than from any ritualistic example inherited from the prior era, and, if we assume, as is usually done, that the earliest exposes published in 1723-25 portrayed the 17th century rituals, we have every reason for believing that the lodge ceremonies were single and simple. Just when the division into two degrees occurred cannot be definitely stated, but it was evidently not before 1719 nor later than 1721, for the Fellow Craft is recognized in the General Regulations of the latter year as having distinctive rank, the terms, Fellow Craft and Master, being used synonymously.

A considerable number of authorities claim to find reliable indications of two degrees or at least the preliminary stages of the division into two degrees prior to 1717, and some claim to find evidence of three. But they do not all rely upon the same evidence, and some repudiate items which others seem to regard as important. Gould, in his *History of Freemasonry* (1885, Vol. 11, p. 67; Vol. III, p. 63) reasoned clearly that but a single ceremony was in use even as late as 1719, but, in his *Concise History of Freemasonry* (1904), following the articles by himself and G. W. Speth in *Ars Quatuor Coronatorum* (1898, 1903), expressed unequivocally the opinion that the Grand Lodge inherited two rudimentary or eroded degrees from the prior era. But his argument of 1904 falls decidedly below that of 1885 in logic, and, indeed, is so inappropriate in parts as to destroy that credence which his unsupported opinion might deserve. For example, he makes the absurd statement that, since the idea that three degrees had existed from early times had permeated the Craft for many years, this idea had perfected its title by legal prescription! Hughan *(Encyclopaedia Britannica*, 1911 ed.) was less inclined to commit himself, saying merely that certain discoveries tended to support the two-degree theory, and citing "Trinity College" MS. ("Free Masonry," Feb., 1911); "Chetwode Crawley" MS. (Grand Lodge Library, Dublin); the Haughfoot minutes; and *History Of Freemasonry* by W. F. Vernon (1893).

Many other writers, not always mutually consistent, have maintained the existence of two or three degrees prior to the Grand Lodge era, basing their arguments on one or more of the following documents: (1) Aitchison's Haven Lodge minutes for 1598; (2) "Sloane" MS. of 1659; (3) "Edinburgh Register House" MS. of date "believed to be" about 1696; (4) "Chetwode Crawley" MS., believed to have been written "about 1730 or earlier"; (5) fragmentary minutes of Haughfoot Lodge for 1702, somewhat qualified by the minutes for 1708; (6) "Trinity College, Dublin" MS., "endorsed 1711"; (7) "Sloane" MS. No. 3329, estimated as of between 1640 and the early 18th century; (8) *A Mason's Examination* of 1723; (9) *The Grand Mystery of Freemasons Discover'd* of 1724; (10) "Briscoe" MS. of 1724-25; (11) Additional MS. No. 23,202 of 1725; (12) "Graham" MS. of 1726; and (13) *A Mason's Confession* of 1727.

Of the foregoing thirteen items, only the first seven are even possibly of the pre Grand Lodge era, and, of those seven, only three, viz., (1), (2), and (5) are certainly of that era, but prove nothing respecting degrees. Some of the remaining four, viz., (3), (4), (6), and (7) would be of considerable significance if they were assuredly of dates before 1717, which they are not; they are only believed to be or, in one instance, endorsed by some unknown person at some unknown time for some unknown reason. A brief comment on these various items follows:

(1) The Aitchison's Haven minutes for 1598 merely show that Entered Apprentices were chosen as intenders for newly entered Apprentices and that Fellow Crafts were chosen as intenders for newly passed Fellow Crafts, which does not necessarily point to any difference in esoteric knowledge between the two ranks any more than would the difference in names, and, since this custom did not appear in other lodges, it would be difficult to explain how two degrees could have been practiced in this lodge and still be so long disregarded by other lodges.

(2) "Sloanc" MS. of 1659 contains nothing of significance respecting degrees and has doubtless been confused with "Sloane" MS. No. 3329 mentioned below.

(3) and (4) "Edinburgh Register House" MS. and "Chetwode Crawley" MS. are similar and are perhaps the principal items now relied on by exponents of an early two-degree system. The former indicates that the person about to "take the word" was first sworn and then went out with the "youngest mason," who instructed him in the manner of giving the "due guard" consisting of the "sign, postures, and the words of his entry." He then reentered the lodge and

gave the words of entry and received the "Mason Word." The MS. then states that "all the signs and words as yet spoken of are only what belong to the entered apprentice," there being others belonging to the Master Mason or Fellow Craft. Thereupon, all but Masters were excluded and the candidate, after taking another oath, returned with the "youngest mason" ("Youngest master" in the "Chetwode Crawley" MS.) and, being similarly instructed as before, returned to make the "master's sign" and give the former words of entry "leaving out the common judge." These MSS. would be quite significant if we knew when they were written.

(5) For some years, the fragmentary Haughfoot minutes for 1702 were the principal evidence relied upon by advocates of the early two-degree system. The incomplete memorandum reads as follows:

> "of entrie as the apprentice did leaving out (the common judge). They then whisper the word as before, and the Master grips his hand in the ordinary way."

Gould attached no importance to this item. While this possibly refers to a second ceremony, it appears that the entry, grip, and word were the same, the only difference being, as also stated in MSS. (3) and (4), that the "common judge" was omitted, and, hence, there was no esoteric distinction sufficient to constitute a degree.

Moreover, the Haughfoot minutes for 1708 show that two apprentices were admitted and received the word "in common form," indicating one word and not two as would be used in separate degrees. Reference to the "common judge" is also found in the "Edinburgh Register House" MS. where it appears that the Entered Apprentice was "sworn by God and St. John by the Square and compass, and common judge." The "jedge" or "jadge" or misspelled as "judge" was a gauge, standard or templet, but why this was omitted as to the Fellow Craft is not clear.

(6) "Trinity College, Dublin" MS. contains this interesting passage:

> "The Masters sign is back bone, the word is matchpin. The fellow craftsman's sign is knuckles, & sinues ye word Jachquin. The Enterprentice's sign is sinues, the word Boaz or its hollow. Squeeze the Master by ye back bone, put your knee between his, & say Matchpin. Squeeze the fellow craftsman in knuckles, & sinues & say Jachquin. Squeeze the enterprentice in sinues, & say boaz, or its hollow."

That, of course, would indicate three degrees in Ireland, but as above stated the date of this MS. is uncertain.

(7) "Sloane" MS. sets forth a form of oath to keep secret the "mason word and everything therein contained," but proves nothing respecting degrees and is of uncertain date.

(8) to (13), inclusive, are all of dates long subsequent to the organization of the Grand Lodge.

To ascribe the early dates which some do ascribe to several of these MSS. would render them mutually inconsistent, for there would then appear to have been a three-degree system in Ireland, a two-degree system in some Scots lodges, and a single ceremony in the rest, including, so far as we know, all English lodges. It would be odd if three degrees were known and practiced as early as 1711 and yet that the Grand Lodge in the metropolis should have been heedless of a third degree until 1725, and rather uncertain about it for some years afterwards. The *Constitutions of 1723* make it abundantly clear that the Fellow Craft was the highest rank contemplated, being qualified to become Master of a lodge or even Grand Master. Though Article XIII of the General Regulations, relating to Quarterly Communications, contained the cryptic clause. "Apprentices must be admitted Masters and Fellows only here, unless by a Dispensation," the two names there used must be taken as synonymous, as they were deemed to be in many quarters even at much later times.

The first unequivocal reference to a Master's Degree is found in the minutes for May 12, 1725 of "Philo-Musicae et Architecturae Societas

Apolloni" which was not a lodge but a society confining its membership to Freemasons. On November 27, of the same year, the Grand Lodge adopted a resolution amending Regulation XIII by providing that "the Master of each lodge, with the consent of his Wardens and the Majority of the Brethren, being Masters may make Masters at their discretion." The well known preeminence of the third degree at the present day renders it difficult to imagine the precarious standing and the little understood character of the Master's Degree in the early 18th century, as to which even Martin Clare seemed decidedly uncertain in 1730 when he delivered his *Defense of Masonry* in which he said: "There is the degree of entered prentice, master of his trade, or fellow craft and master, or the master of the Company." The Irish *Book of Constitutions* of 1730 and the *Pocket Companion* of 1735 refer to only two degrees. The first record of the Master's Degree in a warranted lodge appears in the minutes for 1732 of Lodge No. 83 in London.

Strictly speaking, this degree was unconstitutional in its inception and remained so until recognized in the *Constitutions of 1738,* wherein Dr. Anderson, in many places, changed "Fellow Craft" as it appeared in the edition of 1723 to "Master Mason" to reflect the change brought about by the general acceptance of that degree.

There was reason for some disdain respecting the new degree, for by it a title was conferred briefly which had previously been earned only by installation in the Chair, which in turn must have been preceded by some years of service to the Fraternity. The early restriction placed on the degree was not conducive to its reception as a regular or ordinary step and it was not so regarded for some years. Up to 1738 some entrants were admitted according to the two-degree system, others the three-degree system. The Master's Degree was not worked generally or regarded as necessary until mid century, and, when conferred, was usually worked in bodies separate from the ordinary lodge, called "Master's lodges," of which we hear until well toward the close of the 18th century, the first in America being formed in 1738, the minutes of which are extant to the year 1783. The indiscriminate use of the terms, Master, Passed Master, and Fellow Craft, makes it impossible to say just which degrees were worked in some 18th century lodges.

The Master's Degree in Scotland is first mentioned in the minutes of Canongate Kilwinning Lodge for March 31, 1735, but is not referred to in those of Kilwinning Lodge until 1736 or of Edinburgh until 1738. The Lodges at Aitchison's Haven, Dunblane, Haughfoot, and Peebles were unacquainted with the degree as late as 1760, and the minutes of Lodge of Kelso contain a curious entry showing that the degree was introduced there on June 18, 1754 by visiting Masters from Canongate and Leith. In view of these circumstances, it is not improper to say that, in the first half of the 18th century, the Master's Degree was virtually what was afterwards called, particularly in the United States, a side degree. Its uncertain status, so prolonged, undoubtedly furnished an incentive and some justification for the fabrication of other side or higher degrees, which broke out about 1738-40.

Royal Arch and Royal Order of Scotland

The Royal Arch Degree and the Royal Order of Scotland are first heard of about the same time, the earliest mention of the former being in a book published by Fifield Dassigny at Dublin in 1744 in which the author indicated that the degree had been conferred at York, England, for "some years." Hughan stated that the Royal Order of Scotland had a chapter in London in 1743 and Gould avers that it was heard of in England before it was known in Scotland, having a Grand Master in London as early as 1741.

The Royal Arch almost certainly, and the Royal Order possibly, belong to the class of degrees which sprang up in France between 1737 and 1740, generally termed Hauts Grades. The former is further to be classed as of that division of the Hauts Grades known as the Cryptic type, that is, relating to the discovery of Masonic secrets in the subterranean crypts and vaults under the ruins of Solomon's Temple.

The Royal Order contains two degrees called H. R. D. M. (Harodim or Heredom of Kilwinning) and R. S. Y. C. S. (Rosy Cross) and it, therefore, belongs to the class of Hauts Grades which assert a Scots origin, the name, Harodim or Heredom, indicating a mythical mountain in Scotland, which no one has been able to locate. At the present time, the rituals of these two degrees, Royal Arch and Royal Order do not resemble each other and probably never did. The basic theme of the English Royal Arch and the 13th Degree, Royal Arch of Solomon, of the Scottish Rite are the same but the rituals bear only slight resemblance to each other. The ritual of the Royal Order of Scotland is couched in quaint old rhyme, displaying considerable age, with a British rather than a French flavor. The membership of the Royal Order is strictly limited and, unlike the Royal Arch, has never been included in any other rite or group of degrees.

The first lodge record showing the conferring of the Royal Arch Degree is that of Fredericksburg Lodge in Virginia for December 22, 1753.

York Lodge for some years regularly conferred the Royal Arch as the fourth degree. The Ancient Grand Lodge of England enthusiastically adopted it as the perfection and consummation of the third degree. At the Union of 1813 with the premier or Modern Grand Lodge, the Ancients succeeded in having it declared that pure, ancient Masonry consisted of three degrees, Entered Apprentice, Fellow Craft, and Master Mason (including the Supreme Order of the Holy Royal Arch). Subsequently, the degree was placed under control of a Grand Chapter, the three principal officers of which are the three highest officers of the Grand Lodge. This degree was formerly recognized by the Grand Lodge of Scotland but was subsequently dropped. The degree became very popular in America and has become a part of the York Rite, though most Grand Lodges do not recognize it in this country.

Rituals and Lectures

The existence of three degrees in the early 18th century does not necessarily indicate any marked elaboration of ritual, for a degree may have been conferred very simply and briefly, and it is even probable that such was often the fact. Very little can be said authoritatively about those early workings, for they were entirely unwritten or the manuscripts were unusually well guarded. Indeed, our principal knowledge of the subject comes from the various exposes published frequently after 1723 either by renegade Masons or by those who had succeeded in penetrating the secrecy of the lodge. If even the number of degrees was so little understood by the Craft generally, as above indicated, a heterogeneous working of them by the various lodges cannot be doubted. We have no reason to believe that there ever was simply a Masonic ritual or what might be called the Masonic ritual, but all the evidence points to the fact that there have always been, just as there are now, many Masonic rituals. The founders of the Grand Lodge probably had in their possession one or two and no more of the Gothic Constitutions, and they certainly were familiar with the general, variant forms of working in the lodges as represented by the early exposes. These were always in catechistical form, a mixture of simple architectural or geometric symbolism, brief religious or patriarchal references, and some cryptic language or jargon of a character not now readily understood. Necessarily, some improvement and standardization of these rituals were involved in the process of forming the first two degrees and later the third. This process was probably gradual and not as though some ritualist had set himself to the task of preparing three finished and complete products. Even the exposes seemed to reflect changes, for, up to 1730, all of them mentioned but two degrees, while *Masonry Dissected* of that year clearly spoke of three. The probabilities are that many hands were employed for some thirty or forty years following the organization of the Grand Lodge in adding to the rituals and that this was done quite largely on individual initiative, thereby creating many divergences in different parts of Britain. For this, the old Masters of lodges, who often held office year after year, were chiefly responsible.

The most striking of these innovations was the Legend of Hiram, the origin of which is unknown. Dr. Anderson, in his "history" of Freemasonry prefixed to the *Constitutions of 1723,* barely mentions Hiram and attributes no Masonic importance to that character. The Legend itself probably changed after its first introduction and, strange to say, gradually veered away from the Scriptural account of Hiram's participation in the building of Solomon's Temple, with which the modern Legend does not strictly conform. If the Grand Master of England felt free to instruct the Craft, as he did as late as 1819, that "so long as the Master of any lodge observed exactly the Land-Marks of the Craft, he was at liberty to give the lectures in the language best suited to the character of the lodge over which he presided," we may imagine the greater privileges which must have been assumed during the preceding century.

By 1736, Grand Lodges had been formed and the three-degree system had been adopted in Ireland and Scotland and, by 1750, lodges were working in many countries of Europe, in most of the American Colonies, in Canada, and in the West Indies. Their founders brought their rituals to them from many sources and naturally exhibited considerable variations. These divergencies, becoming fixed in the different nations and states, were virtually ineradicable. It was then too late to unify the rituals even if the Grand Lodge had attempted to do so, which it did not.

William Preston made the first serious attempt at unification in the 1770's, and it is not until that time that we gain any definite and dependable insight into the rituals. His appearance was almost providential, for in him was combined the desire with the ability to perform this task. Somewhat precocious as a child, Preston's literary and linguistic education was stimulated by his employment as a printer's apprentice in Edinburgh and his service as secretary to Thomas Ruddiman, a prominent Latin scholar of the northern metropolis. Upon going to London in 1760, at the age of 18 years, he was employed in the shop of William Strahan, the King's printer, in whose employ he spent the rest of his life as a corrector of the press and was brought into contact with some of the leading literary figures of the time.

Preston was made a Mason in London in 1762 at the age of 20 years, becoming Master of the Lodge at Queen's Head, Holborn a few years later. To enable himself the better to perform his duties, he entered upon an intense study of the rules and ritual of the Society and, by personal exploration and with the assistance of associates, he gathered all the various ritualistic interpretations he could find. Thus, he completed a system of lectures which he delivered at a Masonic meeting at the Miter Tavern in 1774, and, the same year, was elected Master of one of the Four Old Lodges (Antiquity), soon thereafter becoming Deputy Grand Secretary and Master of several other lodges. Preston sought to embellish and unify the rituals and to fix them in permanent form, with the thought that they should be delivered without variation. Part of these objectives he accomplished by virtue of his command of English diction, but his lectures were too long for practical purposes and it is doubtful whether they ever were regularly used anywhere. Their volume was undoubtedly accounted for by the fact that he probably gathered into each lecture the contents of several variant lectures as used in different lodges.

It is to be feared that Dr. Roscoe Pound (*Philosophy of Masonry,* 1915) has been led by his own erudition to over read the record and to attribute to Preston a purpose, particularly in the Fellow Craft Degree, to make knowledge the central point of his system, to constitute Masonry a school of scientific education, and to promote culture through instruction. It is most probable that Preston had no such philosophy or purpose. Dissertations on the seven liberal sciences, including Geometry, had appeared in the Gothic Legends for more than three centuries. The five orders of Architecture are mentioned in the catechistical rituals set forth in the exposes, which began to appear as early as 1723. Mention of the celestial and terrestrial globes are found in lodge records of the early 18th century, at which time, these globes were set in frames on the floor. It can hardly be doubted that the five senses of human nature had found their way into the lectures before Preston was made a Mason, but, in any event, it can hardly be supposed that one of Preston's intelligence would expect the somewhat puerile item on the five senses to add anything to the knowledge of an adult person.

The precise disposition of Preston's lectures is difficult to trace. It is hardly probable that any lodge attempted to adopt them in full, though the rhetorical improvements, which he made in passages already in use by a lodge, may have been involved. Undoubtedly, really old Masters were too set in their ways to make any changes at all. Forty years later, at the Union of 1813 between the Ancient and the Modern Grand Lodges new lectures were prepared by Hemming and Williams which were widely approved and used. The effect of Preston's work on American lodges was delayed by the fact that the American Revolution severed relations between Britain and the Colonies until about 1781, by which time Grand Lodges had begun to be formed in the new States. But the Prestonian working had penetrated the States before the end of the century, for it was espoused by Thomas Smith Webb, first of a line of Masonic lecturers who traveled widely among the lodges for many years. Webb abbreviated and rearranged the Prestonian work and, in 1797, published his *Freemason's Monitor,* which went into many editions and was popular with officers of lodges during most of the following century. By reason of that fact and the changes made in English working in and after 1813, it is probable that American working really represents an older form than most of that in England. For the same reason,

Scots and Irish work is older than the English. In the United States, differences in ritual are those among the several Grand Jurisdictions, but in England the variations are among lodges under the same jurisdiction, and there no less than eight forms of working are current: Emulation, Stability, Oxford, West End, Logic, Bristol, Universal, and North London.

Several attempts have been made to unify rituals in the United States. A convention for that purpose was held at Baltimore, Md., in 1843, which accomplished little, and there was even a dispute afterwards as to the form of working, if any, which the convention had preferred. Between 1860 and 1865, Rob Morris of Kentucky attempted to organize Masons all over the country into what he called "Masonic Conservators," whose purpose it should be to secure the adoption in their various states of a form which Morris had prepared and which he called the "Webb-Preston" work. But there was serious opposition to his methods, which some thought were calculated to invade the authority of the Grand Lodges, while others denied that his suggested form was the true Webb-Preston work.

The rituals of Freemasonry have inspired much speculation and produced an abundant literature, continuing to the present day, which pretends to find in them traces of ancient philosophies, religions, mysteries, and symbolism. How much confidence can be placed in these theories, which are in some degree inconsistent with each other, and how much of the supposed resemblance between the ancient and the modern must be attributed to chance or the inevitable borrowings of one age from another must be left to the judgment of one who cares to pursue that intricate investigation, but, to the realist, much of that kind of exposition appears greatly overdrawn, prejudicial, and imaginary. It must be borne in mind that, however scant the interpretations or explanations contained in the rituals themselves, Grand Lodges, which are the official custodians of Masonic doctrine, have been persuaded to adopt no others. All that glisters is not gold; all that astonishes and mystifies is not Freemasonry.

Ancient Grand Lodge

The Grand Lodge of England According to the Old Institutions, also known as the Ancient Grand Lodge, and sometimes called the Atholl Grand Lodge, because of the long Grand Masterships of the two Dukes of Atholl, father and son, was regarded for many years as the result of the so called "Great Masonic Schism," and accordingly frequently referred to as the "Schismatic Grand Lodge." The investigations of Henry Sadler have shown, however, that it was formed by six lodges, composed of Irish Masons living in England who had never affiliated with the premier Grand Lodge, and was not the consequence of a schism, though it may have been instigated by a feeling that the existing Grand Lodge was somewhat aristocratic. At least it is true that, for many years and in both England and the Colonies, the Ancients paid less heed than did their older rival to a man's worldly wealth and honor. Although the Ancients modeled their Book of Constitutions, called *Ahiman Rezon*, meaning Help to a Brother or A Secretary's Handbook by an Informed Brother, or something of that kind, on that of the older body, they asserted, through their resourceful, contentious, and at times vituperative Grand Secretary, Laurence Dermott, who authored *Ahiman Rezon,* that the original Grand Lodge had abandoned ancient ways, made innovations in Masonry, and become modern, whereas the new body adhered to old customs and perpetuated the only true Masonry.

The differences between the doctrines, customs and ceremonies of the premier Grand Lodge, to which, with its apparent acquiescence, the prefix "Modern" became firmly attached, and those of the newer Ancient Grand Lodge were mostly technical and scarcely apparent to the ordinary observer, or, as Gould remarks, even to the rank and file of the two factions, excepting only that the Ancients regularly conferred the Royal Arch Degree as part of their rites, thus espousing a four-degree form of working. This degree, which Dermott called the "root, heart, and marrow of Masonry, the perfection and consummation of the third degree," was very popular, so that, although it was not officially recognized by the Grand Lodge, there came to be more Masons of that degree among the Moderns than among the Ancients. The Ancients boasted of the greater antiquity and purity of their working, which they asserted invested the initiate with more profound secrets than those possessed by their rivals, with the result that, while an Ancient Mason could visit a Modern lodge, the reverse was not true, unless the visitor was first formally "healed" by proper instruction. The Ancient Grand Lodge never attained quite the standing or numbers enjoyed by the Modern, but it was preferred by the Grand Lodges of Scotland and Ireland, so that all Masonry in the British Isles, excepting that of the premier Grand Lodge, was commonly referred to as the "Ancient York Rite." It is to be remarked that, neither during this period of active rivalry nor at any other time, did the premier Grand Lodge exhibit chagrin or rancor toward competitive bodies, but seemed rather to be entirely satisfied with itself, assuming that, in due time, the others would disappear, which they invariably did. By the close of the 18th century the Ancients were perceptibly gaining on their older rival by reason of several policies: their greater zeal, their claim to antiquity, their less aristocratic bearing, their more liberal warranting of military or travelling lodges, and their working of the Royal Arch Degree.

Union of 1813

But the longer the disaffection lasted, the less the reason for it was understood, and through the Craft generally there was little support for its continuance. Efforts to effect a union, which had begun as early as 1794, gave evidence of success when the Modern Grand Lodge, in 1809, by resolution, admitted the adoption of innovations seventy years previously and decided to return to the "ancient landmarks." After elaborate arrangements and the preparation of detailed Articles of Union, the engineers of the reconciliation hit upon the sagacious plan of electing two royal brothers, the Duke of Sussex and the Duke of Kent, Grand Masters of the Modern and Ancients, respectively. The Articles of Union, having been signed by them and other representatives of the two branches, the hitherto rival bodies came together with the greatest good will on St. John the Evangelist's Day, 1813, and, the two Grand Lodges having been opened in separate rooms, marched into the hall, forming a single body, presided over by the two Dukes. The Articles of Union were read and approved, and the Duke of Kent having withdrawn his name from consideration, the Duke of Sussex was unanimously chosen Grand Master of the "United Grand Lodge of Ancient Freemasons of England." Great pains were taken to reconcile the workings of the prior bodies, so that there should be "but one pure, unsullied system, according to the genuine landmarks, laws and traditions of the Craft," but it is significant of the persistence of the Ancients and somewhat indicative of the merits of the respective systems that the reformed working resembled that of the Ancients more than it did that of the Moderns, and most remarkable of all was the provision in the Articles of Union that:

"II It is declared and pronounced that pure Ancient Masonry consists of three decrees, and no more, viz., those of the Entered Apprentice, the Fellow Craft, and the Master Mason (including the Supreme Order of the Holy Royal Arch)."

Up to the time of the Union, the Moderns had warranted a total of 641 lodges and the Ancients, 359, but, after erasing lapsed lodges, 647 were carried forward on the roll of the United Grand Lodge.

[111]

The Period 1750-1813

At the middle of the 18th century, Free Masonry, in its broadest sense, had become a complex aggregate of ceremonies, themes, and doctrine, and its government was beginning to be dissipated among several widely separated, independent authorities. It did not mean the same thing on the Continent as it did in the British Isles, and the Grand Lodge of England, never a strong administrator, was losing control and, in many instances, influence with lodges abroad.

The period 1750-1813 witnessed several epochal developments, the most significant of which were: (1) The publication of the first books on the doctrine and philosophy of Masonry and the virtual beginning of a Masonic literature; (2) The formulation of the Prestonian lectures; (3) The organization and progress of the Ancient Grand Lodge, and its union, after sixty-two years, with the premier Grand Lodge; (4) The organization and independence of European Grand Lodges; (5) The spread and ultimate systematization of the higher degrees; and (6) The organization and independence of Grand Lodges in the United States. The first three items have been discussed; the last three will be treated in the following pages.

CHAPTER VI

European Masonry

General Character

HE VAGARIES of European Masonry are intricate and difficult to follow, virtually the only profit from attempting to do so being the opportunity to observe philosophically the distortions imposed upon the British institution as it was subjected to alien concepts and aptitudes. Results were not always those logically to be expected. In France, a Roman Catholic country, where Freemasonry had been under the ban of the Church since *In Eminenti* of Pope Clement XII, April 28, 1738, the confusion was social, philosophic, and political rather than religious. In Germany, where the power of the Church had been broken for two centuries, religious questions, though not contests with the Church, plagued the Fraternity well into recent years. The estrangement there was between Christians and Jews, the latter not only not being admitted to membership in many lodges, but even being denied the right to visit if already Freemasons.

Mixture of Craft Masonry with, or its subordination to, the Hauts Grades proceeded throughout the Continent, but there was, in Germany, more evident than elsewhere, a strong undercurrent of attachment to English forms and regulations, except as to sectarianism. Also the Germans had greater respect than did the French for the authority and preeminence of the Grand Lodge of England, though that body seems to have made little effort to exercise its power and, when it did, it often prejudiced the very lodges which had been most loyal to it, probably through indifference or lack of information. The Grand Lodge of England seems to have abandoned, at an early date, all hope of influencing the course of French Masonry and never maintained fraternal relations with it.

Freemasonry was like a tree which, indigenous to the free atmosphere of British institutions and society, grew true to species wherever the Anglo-Saxon carried and propagated it, but, though it flourished and even grew rampant on the Continent of Europe, it there brought forth

THE ARMS OF THE "MODERNS," GRAND LODGE OF ENGLAND

The Arms of ỹ moſt Ancient & Honorable Fraternity
of Free and Accepted Maſons

"ANCIENTS," GRAND LODGE OF ENGLAND.

(From Riley's " Yorkshire Lodges," Edinburgh, Jack & Sons.)

EN LA · FLEURY
ROSE IE

The Most High, Puiβant, and Noble Prince
Charles Lenox, Duke of Richmond & Lenax.
Earl of March and Darnley, Baron of
Setterington, Methuin and Torbolton, Kat
of ij moβt Honourable Order of ij Bath.
GRAND MASTER.
AD 1725.   AL. 5725.

A List of the REGULAR LODGES as CONSTITUTED 'till MARCH 25 1725		
	St. Pauls Churchyard	every other Mond. from ij 2 g of April inclusive
	Knaves Acre	every other Wedn. from ij 2 & of April inclusive
Green Lettice	Brownlow Street Holborn	First Wednesday in every Month
	Weſtminſter	Third Fry day in every Month
	Ivy lane	every other Thurſ. from ij 2 of June inclusive
	Newgate ſreet	Firſt Monday in every Month
	Silver ſtreet	Second & Fourth Wednesday in every Month
	in the Strand	Firſt Fry day in every Month

Printed for & Sold by J. Pine Engraver over againſt
Little Britain end in Aldersgate Street

The Dedication and First Page of Pine's "Engraved List of Lodges
Copied from the original published in 1725.

strange fruit. From the grafting of the Ramsay bud of the chivalric-pagan mystery strain, there sprouted so many variant branches that the old stock was all but completely obscured. So many high degrees sprang up and grew more or less fitfully that historians have despaired of enumerating them. Some became bones of contention over which various bodies of French Masons quarreled for at least a century. In Germany, the Strict Observance, with the mystery and allurement of its "Unknown Superior," held many minds in thraldom until the absurdity and fraud became too apparent to be ignored. The superiority of the Cryptic and Chivalric Rites was so readily accepted on the Continent that there Master Masons were regarded and often regarded themselves as plebeians, subject to the overlordship of the nobility and the high state and military officers who possessed the glittering titles conferred by the numerous councils, chapters, and consistories.

The Germans looked upon Freemasonry with awe, which sometimes degenerated into credulity and superstition; the French embraced it with ardor but thoughtlessly loaded it with pomp and so identified it with politics that the fortunes of the Craft ebbed and flowed with the tides that swept in or swept out monarchies, republics, directorates, consulships, and empires.

From the establishment of the Chapter of Clermont at Paris in 1754 and possibly as early as 1750 and the concurrent rise of the Strict Observance in Germany, the history of European Masonry and the history of the Hauts Grades are almost the same thing. There were few lodges or Grand Lodges on the Continent that did not, at one time or another, give way to the vogue of High Grade Masonry, and many continued to embrace it throughout their careers, which were often short.

The difference between the Anglo-Saxon and the continental character is illustrated by the fact that, while the Hauts Grades were corroding Masonry in Europe, other high degrees were absorbed into the York Rite, with so little ado that not even the times or places of their amalgamation can be determined.

Lodges and Grand Lodges

The nearest we can come to fixing the times of the institution of the earliest lodges on the Continent of Europe is to say that there probably was a lodge at Paris in 1725 and possibly one in Belgium in 1721, both unwarranted. The first foreign lodge warranted was established at Madrid in 1728 by the Duke of Wharton, Grand Master of England, in person. The official engraved list of the Grand Lodge at London for 1732 shows a lodge at Paris but when it was warranted is unknown. Other lodges were warranted as follows: Hamburg, 1733; Holland, 1734; Italy, 1735; Portugal, 1735; Sweden, 1735; Switzerland, 1736; Dresden, 1738; Turkey, possibly, 1738; Poland, 1739; Berlin, 1740; Russia, 1740; Bayreuth, 1741; Austria, 1742; Frankfort, 1743; and Denmark, 1743.

Just when independent Grand Lodges arose in the several nations is difficult to say, for some lodges gradually assumed the title and one or more of the prerogatives of a Grand Lodge, particularly that of warranting subordinate lodges, very little supervision being exercised by the parent body at London and very scant records being kept by anybody. Grand Lodges are supposed to have been formed in France and Germany about 1740-41. The formation of subsequent Grand Lodges can be more definitely fixed, though some were short lived and some were so closely associated with bodies of the higher degrees that their character or identity is in doubt. They were as follows: Holland, 1756; Sweden, 1759; Italy (Naples), 1764; Spain, 1767; Switzerland, 1769; Poland, 1769; Russia, 1776; Austria, 1784; Denmark, 1792; Portugal, 1800-02; Belgium, 1833; Greece, 1867; and Norway, 1905.

Hauts Grades

This French term describes the high degrees which began to appear about 1738-40 and which spread over Europe and later into other lands. The origin of these degrees, of which there was a great number, and to many of which the adjective "Scots" or "Scottish" was prefixed, is not well understood, except that it is admitted that none of them arose in Scotland. This fabrication of new degrees is generally agreed to have been suggested by a charge delivered to some candidates in a lodge at Paris in 1737 by the Chevalier Andrew Michael Ramsay, who bore the title of Grand Chancellor, and whose address has been epitomized in Chapter II. Ramsay's theme was novel, the first chivalric, knightly, or military note that had been sounded in Freemasonry, which had universally been deemed to have solely an architectural background, that is to say, a trade, and consequently of an entirely different social rank from that of the nobility and certainly having no connection with military operations, Christian or otherwise.

French imagination seized upon the innovation so avidly that, within three years, the fabrication of Christian, Military, and Chivalric degrees was well under way, of which type Rose Croix and Knight Kadosh in the French system and Knight

Templar in the English are examples. But there was another class, which was suggested by Ramsay's reference to the Knight-Masons who worked with the trowel in one hand and the sword in the other, together with the theme, later added, that while engaged in exploring the underground crypts and vaults of the Temple ruins, they had discovered the true, profound secrets of Freemasonry, hidden for ages and, therefore, unknown to the ordinary Master Mason, who possessed only those of the English Craft system. The degrees resulting from this theme were called variously, Cryptic, Ineffable, and Scots Master, of which, Perfect Elu in the French degrees and Royal Arch in both the French and English systems, and Select Master, transferred from the French to the English rite, are examples. In France, a Scots Master was deemed to outrank even the Master of a symbolic lodge, and, eventually, Scots Directories were formed to govern the affairs of lodges. A Scots Master lodge was set up at Hamburg as early as 1741, and, in the same year, a Kadosh degree appeared at Lyons.

It is supposed that the York Rite degrees of Chivalric and Cryptic types, such as Knight Templar and Royal Arch, were English adaptations of French prototypes. Hughan is authority for the statement that a chapter of the Royal Order of Scotland, consisting of the degrees of

Heredom and Rosy Cross, was established at London in 1743. The Royal Arch is first mentioned in Fifield Dassigny's *Serious and Impartial Enquiry etc.* in 1744 as having been worked for some time at York.

Just why Scotland was honored by use of the term, "Scots" or "Scottish," for many of the higher degrees has never been fully explained. None of them originated there or was worked in that country until the 19th century. Equally perplexing are such names as Royal Order of Heredom and Rose Croix of Heredom, asserted to be greatly venerated in Scotland, and also references in old manuscripts to the mythical "Mount Heredom" in Scotland. To these problems, is added that of the Jacobite flavor possessed by some of the Hauts Grades, supposedly representing Scots influence, since the House of Stuart had many followers in Scotland. A great variety of theories have evolved from the several Scots legends, fables, and romances, revolving around the names of David I of Scotland, Robert Bruce, James, Lord Steward of Scotland, and the Young Pretender, and even such natural objects as the mythical "Mount Heredom." Also they hovered about Kilwinning Lodge, treating it as the center from which all this class of degrees had sprung, though the fact is that that Lodge never worked any but the three

Craft degrees. Whether by Ramsay's reference of 1737 to the refuge of the Templars in Scotland or by some personal influence of Ramsay later exerted or because of some Jacobite effort to curry favor with Scotsmen, the name Scots or Scottish clung to many of the French degrees and to this day describes all that remain of that group, except those which became anglicized and incorporated into the York Rite.

First in France and then in Germany, degrees of the Scots Master, Cryptic, Chivalric, and Philosophical varieties multiplied rapidly, so that, by the middle of the 18th century, they were widely dispersed and had assumed group forms in possession of various lodges, chapters, councils, and even individuals. Among the more prominent of these, was the Rite of Perfection, consisting of 25 degrees as follows: (1) Apprentice; (2) Fellow Craft; (3) Master; (4) Secret Master; (5) Perfect Master; (6) Intimate Secretary; (7) Intendent of the Building; (8) Provost and Judge; (9) Elu of the Nine; (10) Elu of the Fifteen; (11) Illustrious Elect, Chief of the Twelve Tribes; (12) Grand Master Architect; (13) Royal Arch of Solomon; (14) Grand Elect Ancient Perfect Master; (15) Knight of the Sword; (16) Prince of Jerusalem; (17) Knight of the East and West; (18) Knight Rose Croix; (19) Grand Pontiff; (20) Grand Patriarch; (21) Grand Master of the Key of Masonry; (22) Prince Libanus; (23) Sovereign Prince Adept Chief of the Grand Consistory; (24) Illustrious Knight Commander of the Black and White Eagle; and (25) Most Illustrious Sovereign Prince of Masonry, Grand Knight, Sublime Commander of the Royal Secret.

French Masonry

The Chapter of Clermont, set up at Paris in 1754, was, some four years later, absorbed by the Emperors of the East and West (1758-1780), between which and the Knights of the East (1756-1767), a less aristocratic body, rivalry prevailed until the latter succumbed to the edict of the French government in 1767, disbanding the Grand Lodge of France, a step taken, not because of any deliberate opposition to Freemasonry, but as a police measure to quench the wrangling which had then existed for five or six years in the Grand Lodge.

Contributing to the confusion was the institution of the "patent," a French innovation and a novelty in Masonry, by which the holder could personally and privately and without any formal ceremony, pass along to others of his choice the various ranks and titles as authorized by the patent, thus, constituting a radical departure from the original or British method of conferring degrees only in a duly warranted and opened lodge.

It seems that, at a joint meeting between one faction of the Grand Lodge of France and the Emperors, held in 1761, the celebrated patent was issued to Etienne (Stephen) Morin, empowering him to establish bodies of the Rite of Perfection in America, with consequences later to be noted. The following year, the *Constitutions of 1762,* governing that Rite, were adopted. With the death of the Duc de Clermont in 1771, his Grand Lodge virtually expired and, after two years of great confusion, was succeeded in 1773 by the "Grand Lodge," consisting of Paris Masters, and the "National Grand Lodge at the Orient of Paris," later called the "Grand Orient." Both bodies purported to confine themselves to Craft Masonry, but by 1786 both had affiliated with themselves chapters of the high degrees, that of the Grand Orient being the abbreviated Rite of Perfection known as "Rit Moderne" or French Rite. The two bodies reached their greatest prosperity just before the French Revolution, the Grand Lodge having on its rolls 88 Paris and 43 provincial lodges, and the Grand Orient, 67 Paris lodges and 539 in the colonies, provinces, and military forces, but counting the various bodies of the higher degrees the total was about 900.

Among the more curious orders of the time were the "Scots Philosophic Rite" (1766-1818), the "Philalethes" (1771-1792), and the Philadelphians (1780-1810), all aspiring to intellectual attainments and composed of some of the most learned men of the age, who participated in the study and discussion of a wide range of subjects. The first named body possessed a library of over 2000 volumes.

The French Revolution, which broke out in 1789 and reached its culmination in the Terror of 1793-94, interrupted all Masonic activities, extinguished some bodies, and resulted in the deaths of many Paris Masters. The Duc d'Orleans, Grand Master of the Grand Orient, though attempting to save himself by renouncing the Order, was beheaded in November 1793. In 1795-6, the Grand Lodge and Grand Orient revived, and, three years later, the two bodies combined as the Grand Orient, but the old tendency of aberration again asserted itself. In 1804, Hacquet brought his Rite of Perfection from New York and de Grasse-Tilly, his Ancient and Accepted Scottish Rite of 33 Degrees from Charleston, S. C. For some years French Masonry was aligned with political trends and disgracefully obsequious to influences of state. The Scottish Rite appointed Louis Buonaparte, brother of the Emperor, to be Grand Master, and the Grand Orient retaliated by selecting both the Emperor's brothers, Louis and Joseph, and Marshal Murat for its highest officers. After some preliminary skirmishing, an agreement was reached whereby the Grand Orient would control the first 18 Degrees, and the Scottish Rite, the rest of the 33. In 1805, Joseph Buonaparte became Grand Master of the Grand Orient and Cambaceres, one of the three Consuls under the Constitution of 1799, became his deputy, the latter, in the following year, becoming also Grand Commander of the Scottish Rite and Honorary Grand Master of the Royal Order of Scotland. All rites being under the direction of one man, peace seemed assured. But, in 1813, de Grasse-Tilly returned to claim his old authority, and, with the restoration of the Monarchy in 1814, French Masonry fawned upon royalty, deposed its former officers, and accepted General Beurnonville as its head. All this had to be reversed upon Napoleon's return from Elba in 1815, and re-reversed only three months later following the debacle at Waterloo. The Grand Orient was now locked in a struggle with the Supreme Council, which in turn disputed authority with three other putative councils, and for some years both the Grand Orient and the Supreme Council claimed authority over the whole scale of 33 Degrees. Two new bodies, the Rite of Misraim and the Rite of Memphis (1838) appeared on the scene.

In 1848, the Grand Orient was reorganized and placed under the administration of a Constituent Assembly, headed by a President, and a very significant change was made in religious doctrine, it being declared that "Freemasonry has for its principles the existence of Deity and the immortality of the soul," the Grand Orient having, prior to this time, followed the negative attitude on religion manifested by the English *Constitutions of 1723.* A "National Grand Lodge," espousing certain reforms, was organized in 1848 but the police at the instance of the Grand Orient and the Supreme Council closed it two years later. When Louis Napoleon became Emperor the confusion in the Grand Orient was so great that Prince Louis Murat was made Grand Master and ruled with an iron hand, bringing the Grand Orient under complete subservience to him and the government. His most notable act was an attempt to assemble a universal Masonic Congress at Paris in 1855, but this was poorly attended and accomplished nothing. Following the disclosure of scandal and the return of intramural quarreling, the Emperor, Louis Napoleon, took control of the situation in 1862 and appointed Marshal Magnan Grand Master. In 1867 the Grand Orient gave recognition to the revived Council of the Scottish Rite in Louisiana, which claimed authority over the Craft Degrees, thus threatening to transfer to this country the confusion existing in France. In response to the appeal of the Grand Lodge of Louisiana for aid, some 25 or 30 Grand Lodges in the United States severed relations with the Grand Orient.

In 1869 the Grand Orient resolved that neither color, race, nor religion would disqualify an applicant for the degrees, which, although it conformed strictly to Masonic doctrine, aroused resentment in some quarters of the United States. In 1871 the Grand Orient abolished the office of Grand Master and conferred those duties on the President of a council, which was regarded as a serious departure from Masonic practice. Finally, in 1877, the Grand Orient again amended its constitution to provide, in lieu of belief in God and immortality, that Masonry had for its basis "absolute liberty of conscience and the solidarity of humanity," to omit from its ritual all reference to God, and to make the display of the Bible optional with the lodges. This called forth much denunciation from English speaking Masons, and later writers have commonly said that such action was the cause for the severance of relations between the Grand Orient and Grand Lodges in the United

States. But the fact is that most Grand Lodges in this country had either never established fraternal relations with the Grand Orient or had terminated them years earlier.

German Masonry

By 1751, there had been established in Germany a Provincial Grand Lodge at Hamburg, Union Lodge at Frankfurt, a Grand Lodge at Dresden, the Lodge of the Three Globes at Berlin, Sun Lodge at Bayreuth, and lodges in East Prussia. The first two were of pure English ancestry, but the lodges at Berlin and Bayreuth were formed under some sort of claimed royal prerogative. The Grand Lodge of the Three Swords at Dresden was the first independent Grand Lodge in Germany. From time to time there existed in that country about 15 Grand Lodges, all but 8 of which expired, the survivors being the following: (1) Grand Lodge of Hamburg, which became independent of England in 1811 and which had at that time 12 subordinate lodges; (2) Mother Grand Lodge of the Eclectic Union at Frankfurt, which, though it had received inconsiderate treatment, remained true to the London body until 1823 when it became independent; (3) Grand National Mother Lodge of the Three Globes, which was never under English warrant, but which assumed Grand Lodge prerogatives as early as 1744 and finally became one of the most influential Masonic bodies in Germany; (4) National Grand Lodge of Saxony at Dresden, a revival in 1811 of the old Grand Lodge of the Three Swords, which had been virtually absorbed by the Strict Observance in 1762; (5) Grand Lodge of the Sun at Bayreuth, which was formed in 1811 with four lodges; (6) National Grand Lodge of All German Freemasons at Berlin, which, though its title was somewhat exaggerated, did finally become the second largest in Germany. It was the creation of Count Zinnendorff, a somewhat unscrupulous organizer who had dabbled in practically all of the systems of Hauts Grades and who, about 1770, simply seceded from the Swedish system, taking 12 lodges with him and declaring the existence of his new Grand Lodge. His resourcefulness is illustrated by the fact that he procured the Grand Lodge of England to recognize his creature as the only constituent power in Germany, except Frankfurt and Brunswick, which were to be allowed to lapse. Frederick the Great patronized this Grand Lodge, which was so extremely arrogant that the Grand Lodge of England withdrew recognition in 1788; (7) Grand Lodge of Prussia or Royal York of Friendship, which was an offshoot of the Three Globes, and enjoyed the especial favor of the Grand Lodge of England, because it had initiated the Duke of York in 1765, who became its patron and gave it the name, Royal York. It became actually independent in 1768. (8) Grand Lodge of Concord at Darmstadt, which was erected in 1846.

In Germany, the Hauts Grades assumed forms somewhat weird, led by the Strict Observance in the hands of Baron von Hund, a man of education and apparently of honor but credulous to an unfortunate degree. The central theme of this rite, which consisted of six degrees, was that implicit and unquestioning obedience be given to the "Unknown Superior" or "Knight of the Red Feather," whose identity was hidden even from von Hund but who was suspected to be either Lord Kilmarnock or the Young Pretender. The Strict Observance swept through Germany where, for a while, it practically superseded the English Craft Rite. It invaded France in 1774 and traveled to Italy, Switzerland, Russia, Holland, and Denmark, surviving in the last named country until 1855. Several other rites or groups of degrees made considerable headway, such as that formed by Count Zinnendorff, von Koppen's African Architects, Count Schemettau's Rite, the Gold Rosicrucians, and the Illuminati. The two last named were really not Masonic, but attracted some Masons, adopted degree systems, and became more or less identified with Masonry in the popular

THE
NEW BOOK
OF
CONSTITUTIONS
OF THE
Antient and Honourable Fraternity
OF
FREE and ACCEPTED MASONS.

CONTAINING

Their *History, Charges, Regulations,* &c.

COLLECTED and DIGESTED

By Order of the GRAND LODGE from their old *Records,*
faithful *Traditions* and *Lodge-Books,*

For the Use of the LODGES.

By JAMES ANDERSON, D. D.

LONDON:

Printed for Brothers CÆSAR WARD and RICHARD CHANDLER,
Bookfellers, at the *Ship* without *Temple-Bar* ; and fold at their
Shops in *Coney-Street,* YORK, and at SCARBOROUGH-SPAW.
M DCC XXXVIII.

In the *Vulgar* Year of Mafonry 5738.

TO THE

Moft *High, Puiffant* and moft *Illuftrious* PRINCE

FRIDERICK LEWIS,

Prince *Royal* of GREAT-BRITAIN,
Prince and Stewart of SCOTLAND,

PRINCE of WALES,

Electoral Prince of Brunswick-Luneburg,
Duke of *Cornwall, Rothfay,* and *Edinburgh,*
Marquis of the Ifle of *Ely,*
Earl of *Chefter* and *Flint, Eltham* and *Carrick,*
Vifcount *Launcefton,*
Lord of the *Ifles, Kyle* and *Cunningham,*
Baron of *Snaudon* and *Renfrew,*
Knight of the moft noble Order of the Garter,
Fellow of the *Royal* Society,
A *Mafter* MASON, and *Mafter* of a LODGE.

GREAT SIR,

The Title Page and Dedication of the "New Book of Constitutions," by James Anderson, D. D.

Copied from the original published in 1738.

York Cathedral.

MEDIÆVAL CATHEDRAL ARCHITECTURE IN ENGLAND.

mind, considerably injuring the older institution. The confusion occasioned by the Hauts Grades afforded a favorable environment for the operations of two celebrated charlatans, Gugumos and Cagliostro, the latter being the creator of the "Egyptian Rite."

Toward the end of the 18th century, in Germany where there had always been an element opposed to the Hauts Grades, the work of two reformers, Schroeder and Fessler, gradually produced renewed vigor in Craft Masonry. Most of the vagaries languished and the Zinnendorff Rite migrated to Sweden and, in somewhat modified form, became the Swedish Rite.

Modern European Masonry

The European Fraternity has been subjected to many vicissitudes well into modern times and, toward the middle of the 20th century, experienced cataclysmic misfortunes. The Church of Rome has everywhere opposed it and its treatment at the hands of monarchs has varied from approval to complete prohibition, either attitude being sometimes reversed by successive monarchs. It was not seriously disturbed by World War I, and, indeed, French Masonry was elevated in the eyes of American Masons, due to the high character of the French Fraternity and the opportunity which American Masons in the expeditionary forces had to become acquainted with it. But, during the two decades following that struggle, there was a great upsurge of dictatorial government, particularly in Italy, Spain, Germany, and Russia, in all of which, except the last named, in which Freemasonry had not existed for the preceding century, the Society was persecuted and its members driven into exile or murdered.

Strangely enough, in Germany where the Jews had been somewhat discriminated against by the Fraternity, the Nazi linked Freemasons and Jews together and persecuted first one and then the other for the alleged faults of one or the other or for an asserted conspiracy between them. Even the Temples, who were often of architectural elegance and expensively furnished, were despoiled and their contents set up as museums to which gaping crowds were admitted to wonder and deride. In Italy and Spain the persecuting agencies did not pause to sneer but proceeded immediately with the liquidation of Masons and Masonic bodies. The Supreme Council of Spain went into exile in Mexico and the Grand Lodge of London provided sanctuary for several Grand Lodges, which were driven into exile during World War II.

European Masonry since World War II

THE unquenchable thirst for the freedom of man's choice to think for himself finally prevailed - for a time - with the end of Fascism, Nazism, Communism and the Berlin Wall culminating with the Gulf War. Freemasonry and its members suffered so much during the dark days of suppression by plundering, confiscation and closing of lodges and the torture and annihilation of members. From the embers and ashes of such carnage rose the flickering attributes of truth, hopes and steadfastness - Freemasonry's lesson in FORTITUDE.

Grand Lodges from various middle Europe which had gone into exile again took form through the help of Grand Lodges in more stabilized countries: Italy, France, England, Germany, Canada, and the United States. The Grand Lodge of Belgium founded in 1979 had 24 lodges in 1994. The Grand Lodges of Poland and Portugal were reactivated in 1990-1991. Russia had 2 lodges.

But, what has happened? In 1973, The Islamic World Conference succeeded in having Freemasonry banned in Islamic countries. Russia, while trying to achieve democracy has been divided in separate countries, each vying to reach its place in the world and maintaining autonomy. Yugoslavia so hopefully reorganized its Grand Lodge in 1991. Will it survive? It has divided itself into 4 separate countries committing civil strife with the loss of many lives. Unrest continues between Serbia and Croatia. What of the Grand Lodge of Romania founded by the Grand Lodge of Italy in 1993? The Grand Lodge of Czechoslovakia was reactivated in 1990. Dissension has caused that country to split and there are now two countries: Czech and Slovakia.

For more details see Coil's Revised 1996 *Encyclopedia* under each country and also each country under Anti-Masonry.

CHAPTER VII

Freemasonry in the United States

Beginnings of Freemasonry in America

SINCE THE UNITED STATES has come to have approximately one-half of the Grand Lodges and two thirds of the Freemasons in the world, the events attending the introduction of Freemasonry into this country are of great significance. In this regard as in others, Masonic writers have endeavored to antiquate Masonic activities as much as possible and sometimes more than probable. An example of this tendency is the story of the "Nova Scotia Stone," which was found some years ago and which bore very clearly the numerals, "1606." The stone was subsequently lost but, fortunately, before that event, it had been photographed. In some way, the rumor spread that it bore Masonic symbols and thus indicated the work of some member of the Craft. Some imaginative person expanded that statement to say that the stone bore the square and compasses, and this has even crept into publications of pretended accuracy. The fact is easily observable from the photographs that, while there are vague markings on the stone, they bear not the slightest resemblance to any Masonic symbol, much less the square and compasses. Then there was the claim that a manuscript existed showing that some Jews had opened a lodge in Rhode Island in 1656 or 58 and had conferred the degrees of Masonry on one of their race. The deficiencies in this story should have been apparent, viz., that at the time stated, Freemasonry was nominally Trinitarian Christian in doctrine, and there were no degrees such as were conferred in later years when this manuscript, if it ever existed, was probably written.

It is now generally agreed that John Skene, a member of Aberdeen Lodge, Scotland, who came to Burlington, New Jersey, in 1682, was the first Freemason known to have been in this country. This fact renders unimportant the dubious case of John Moore, Collector of the Port of Philadelphia, who is supposed to have written a letter, not now preserved, recounting a meeting with his Masonic brethren in 1715.

The first well-known, and long supposed to have been the first Freemason in the Colonies was Jonathan Belcher, who became Governor of the Colony of Massachusetts and New Hampshire, and whose written statement, made in 1741, is preserved to the effect that he had been a Mason for thirty-seven years, thus placing his admittance in 1704 when he is known to have been in England. It has been asserted that the title papers to King's Chapel in Boston contained evidence that a lodge of Freemasons was held there in 1720, but that evidence is not preserved. The fact that Boston News Letter for May 25, 1727 contained an account of the Communication of the Grand Lodge at London in that year indicated that the editor knew of persons in Boston to whom this would be of interest. Lord Baltimore was made a Mason in England in 1730, but there is no indication that he promoted Masonry in Maryland.

The first official act of the Grand Lodge of England respecting the American Colonies was the deputation issued, June 5, 1730, to Daniel Coxe as Provincial Grand Master for New York, New Jersey and Pennsylvania. This is preserved in the records of the Grand Lodge, but although Coxe came to New Jersey, where he was judge of the Colonial Court, there is nothing to indicate that he ever exercised his authority or took part in any Masonic activities here.

The presence of a considerable number of Freemasons in Philadelphia as early as 1730 is indicated by Benjamin Franklin's publication, in his "Philadelphia Gazette" for December 8, 1730, of one of the exposes of Masonry, then current in England, accompanied by the statement that there were "several Lodges of Free Masons erected in this Province, and People have lately been much amus'd with Conjectures concerning them." That Franklin, not then a Mason, became one within two months thereafter is shown by a certain "Libre B," the oldest Colonial Lodge document now preserved. It contains the accounts of a lodge which met at the Tun Tavern in Philadelphia, the entry for June, 1731, showing that Franklin's dues were charged back five months. It indicates meetings almost every month from June 24, 1731 to June 1737, and, after a lapse of one year, the last meeting in June 1738. This lodge, which seems to have had 14 members in June 1731, undoubtedly had met for some time prior to that year, and, during the seven years covered by the record, the names of 48 individual members appear. It was an "immemorial rights" lodge, that is, it held no warrant of authority from the Grand Master in Britain but acted pursuant to the Old Charges, which it had the right to do, unless its members had in some way become subject to the authority of the Grand Lodge of England. Such lodges were not unknown, even at later times, for Fredericksburg Lodge in Virginia, where George Washington was made a Mason in 1752, did not receive its charter from the Grand Lodge of Scotland until 1758. The characterization of such lodges as "irregular" by some writers is the unjustifiable result of anachronistic thinking, that is, reasoning in the light of rules or conditions which did not exist until later times. The old Lodges at York and Alnwick, England, remained independent for many years, and the authority of the Grand Lodge of England was not universally recognized in that country until well toward the close of the 18th century, irrespective of those lodges which were under the rival Grand Lodge of Ancients.

Upon the departure of William Button, Master of the Tun Tavern Lodge, William Allen succeeded him in 1731, and proceeded to form a Grand Lodge, which makes it necessary to explain that the terms, Grand Master and Grand Lodge, were then used in other than their present meaning, viz., to indicate jurisdiction over Masons generally in the community as distinguished from members of a private lodge alone. It was not a representative body composed of officers or delegates from subordinate or constituent lodges.

On April 30 (or 13), 1733, Viscount Montague, Grand Master of England, by deputation, constituted Henry Price, a member of Lodge No. 75, which met at the Rainbow Coffee House, London, Provincial Grand Master of New England, and on July 30, 1733, Price opened his Grand Lodge at the Bunch of Grapes Tavern in King's Street, Boston, appointed Andrew Belcher, son of Jonathan Belcher, Deputy and pursuant to petition from 18 brethren, formed them into a lodge, known for many years as "First Lodge," which bore No. 126 on the register of the Grand Lodge of England. This lodge, after some years, by amalgamation with other lodges, became "St. John's Lodge" and has had continuous existence to the present day. On January 2, 1738/9, a "Master's Lodge" was formed, followed by "Second Lodge" and "Third Lodge" in 1749/50. Price later claimed jurisdiction over all of North American under an asserted "order" of Lord Crawford in 1734, but since Price's successor, Robert Tomlinson, was deputized in 1736 for New England only, the wider jurisdiction is not probable prior to the appointment in 1743 of Thomas Oxnard as Provincial Grand Master for North America. Price's claim and the fact that Benjamin Franklin, as Grand Master at Philadelphia, by letter in 1734, sought information as to the rumored extension of Price's authority, looking to the possibility of securing a warrant for the Philadelphia body, has occasioned considerable dispute, it being claimed by exponents of Boston's primacy that such warrant was issued, as reported in the public press. The fact that one Provincial Grand Master had no power to deputize another Provincial Grand Master lends grave doubt to the claim. In 1737, a wave of anti-Masonic agitation swept through Pennsylvania, and the Tun Tavern Lodge suspended work for about 12 years. In 1749, Pennsylvania Masonry revived and Franklin accepted an appointment as Provincial Grand Master from Oxnard, who had become Provincial Grand Master for North America in 1743. For the reasons above stated, this was obviously irregular and appears to have been so considered at the time, for William Allen applied to Lord Byron, Grand Master of England, for a warrant, which was granted March 13, 1749/50, and Franklin became Allen's Deputy.

In 1752, dissention arose at Boston, which lasted for 40 years, with important repercussions on Massachusetts Masonry. In that year, a lodge of unknown composition began to meet at the Green Dragon Tavern, and two years later a petition for a charter was sent to the Grand Master of Scotland, which was received in 1760 authorizing "St. Andrew's Lodge." The older body refused to have fraternal relations with it, with the result that the rejected body applied for, and, in 1769, received from Scotland a warrant for a Provincial Grand Lodge, with Dr. Joseph Warren as Grand Master in Boston and within 100 miles thereof. In 1773 this jurisdiction was extended to the whole Continent of America.

Boston and Philadelphia became the two foci from which Masonry spread through the Colonies, though not without important contributions from other Provincial Grand Lodges and through warrants directly from Britain. The greatest activity of Philadelphia Masonry in this respect was after its conversion to Ancient allegiance, the first lodge (No. 69) of that variety having been warranted there in 1758 and a Provincial Grand Lodge, with William Ball as Provincial Grand Master, on July 15, 1764 (No. 89 with priority of 1761), both by the Grand Lodge of Ancients. It has to be remembered that there were two systems of Freemasonry in both the British Isles and the Colonies during the second half of the 18th century, and that, though the distinctions between them were often not understood by the Craft generally, the division was marked and had its effect upon events.

The following table shows, for the respective Colonies, the years in which immemorial rights lodges are known to have first met, and the years in which warranted lodges and Provincial Grand

Lodges were first established by the Moderns and the Ancients, respectively:

Colony	Imm.rights Lodge	Warranted Lodges Modern	Ancient	Provincial G.L.'s Modern	Ancient
Massachusetts		1733	1756	1733	1769
Georgia	1733	1735	1784		
South Carolina		1735-6	1764	1736	
New Hampshire	1736-9	1739	1780		
Virginia	1752	1741(?)	1758		
Pennsylvania	1730	1749/50	1758	1749/50	1761-4
Rhode Island		1749			
Maryland	1749	1750	1766		
Connecticut		1750	1781		
New York	1738-9	1753	1776	1751	1781
North Carolina		1754	1766	1771	
New Jersey		1761	1767		
Delaware		1765	1769		

The American Revolution

The American Revolution had a marked and lasting effect on Freemasonry in the Colonies and in the new States. One result was the advancement of Ancient Masonry as compared with Modern Masonry. Although twenty-three years elapsed between the warranting of the first Modern and the first Ancient lodges in the Colonies and although the institution of Ancient lodges and Provincial Grand lodges everywhere lagged many years behind the organiza-

[**142**]

tion of Modern bodies, the conclusion of the Revolution found the two of almost equal influence. The older or Modern lodges, especially in the larger centers of population, were disposed to be somewhat aristocratic, or at least they paid some attention to a man's worldly wealth and honor, which resulted in no little dissatisfaction, followed by the establishment of Ancient lodges at Boston and Philadelphia as early as 1756 and 1758 respectively. Army lodges helped to advance or to publicize Ancient Masonry, and at Boston and New York they even participated in organizing Ancient Provincial Grand Lodges. Military lodges began to arrive with British regiments as early as the French and Indian War of 1755 and increased in numbers as the Revolution approached. The Grand Lodges of Ireland and Scotland had warranted by far the greater number of these and the Ancient Grand Lodge of England, all of the Ancient persuasion. The outstanding effect of the Revolution, however, was the erection, beginning even during the hostilities, of independent Grand Lodges in all of the Colonies or States, which at the end of another century had increased to 49, extending across the Continent to the Pacific Coast and constituting about half of the Grand Lodges in the world.

A great deal has been spoken and written about the part which Freemasonry played in the Revolution, and the desire of some to cover the Fraternity with glory from a nationalistic stand point has led them almost to give the impression that this great adventure was a Masonic project. Such misrepresentation has had unfortunate consequences, for non-Masonic writers have adopted this text to depict Freemasonry as a revolutionary and political instrumentality. A recent example is *Revolution and Freemasonry* by Bernard Fäy, wherein, by labored argument and unjustifiable surmise and inference, the author endeavored to fasten upon the Fraternity responsibility for both the American and the French Revolutions. Also, following World War 1, General von Ludendorff and later Hitler conducted persecutions of the German Fraternity, along with the Jews, charging that they had conspired to betray their Country and cause the loss of the war by disclosing the plans of the German General Staff.

The fancy that, in war or other national or international crises or on political questions generally, Freemasons are all or almost all on one side is completely fallacious. Freemasons are found on both sides, and, so far as anyone knows, they are divided on all such questions in about the same proportions, as is the general public. It involves a gross misunderstanding of history to suppose that the people of the

Colonies unanimously or almost unanimously supported revolt. They were divided for innumerable reasons, business, financial, economic, and social. The upper classes tended to be Tory and opposed to revolt, while farmers, mechanics, and the working classes were more demonstrative, there being, of course, many exceptions to the rule on both sides. We know that the people of Britain were not all opposed to the Colonial cause and that such statesmen as Burke and Pitt openly espoused it.

There is no evidence that the lodges or Freemasons, as such, generally manifested revolutionary sentiments, though individuals exhibited various degrees of ardor for one side or the other. In all probability, the members of lodges were of mixed emotions but suppressed them in their fraternal relations. Families are often divided on such questions, and there is no reason why Masons should not be. For example, in old First Lodge at Boston, there was James Otis, whose voice was raised against oppression fifteen years before the Declaration of Independence, and who is sometimes referred to as the "Counsellor of the Revolution," though "Herald of the Revolution" would be equally appropriate. In 1761 he attacked the right of the Crown to issue writs of assistance or search warrants, and though he lost the case in court his name is lustrous in American history. But in the same lodge there was Jeremy Gridley, the King's Attorney General, who prevailed over Otis in that trial. In Second Lodge there was Gridley's younger brother, Richard, who was in the Colonial army and was the engineer who laid out the fortifications for the defense of Boston.

All but one of the Provincial Grand Masters of the older or Modern Masonic establishments in the Colonies were Tories, and undoubtedly a large part of the Craft were like minded, else those officers would not have long retained their positions. Moreover, it is the common fault of Masonic writers on this subject to forget the fact that the Tories conformed to one of the fundamental principles of Masonry, embodied in all constitutions and regulations for the past five centuries, from the Ancient Charges to the present day, that Masons shall be loyal to the king or to the civil government under which the Fraternity exists. The restriction on the discussion of political issues in the lodge is equally well known. We have no reason to believe that these teachings were disregarded in Colonial times any more than they are now.

At the outbreak of hostilities there were seven Provincial Grand Lodges in the Colonies, five Modern (Massachusetts, Pennsylvania, New York, North Carolina, and South Carolina)

The old Tun Tavern, Philadelphia.

IN WHICH THE FIRST LODGE OF FREEMASONS WAS ORGANIZED IN NORTH AMERICA.

Green Dragon Tavern, Boston, Mass., in 1773.

and two Ancient (Massachusetts and Pennsylvania). At Boston, John Rowe of the Moderns was a Tory or at least indifferent to the Colonial cause. He was a merchant and shipper and, for that reason and because of his coolness toward revolt, he was, on several occasions, openly insulted on the streets of Boston. Thomas Brown, Secretary of First and Second Lodges, departed for Nova Scotia, taking the lodge records with him, at the time the British evacuated Boston. Joseph Warren of the Ancients was an ardent patriot. In Pennsylvania, William Allen of the Moderns was a Tory and put himself under the protection of Lord Howe, who held possession of Philadelphia. One of the Ancient lodges there suspended and the other lost two of its officers, who went over to the British. The attitude of the Provincial Grand Master of the Ancients in Pennsylvania is unknown. In New York, Sir John Johnson of the Moderns, together with several lodge officers, fled to Canada, and Sir John commanded the King's forces in western New York throughout the War. Joseph Montfort, Provincial Grand Master of the Moderns in North Carolina and his Deputy, Cornelius Harnett, were prominent in Colonial counsels throughout the Revolution. Edgerton Leigh of the Moderns in South Carolina fled to England. So the picture of a Masonic revolution has been considerably overdrawn.

Very great latitude has been taken by numerous writers in declaring who were Freemasons in Revolutionary times, and, aided by the dearth of lodge records, they have indulged in considerable surmise so as to attribute membership on those whose patriotic or political records they regard as creditable to the Fraternity. Such statements are made as that virtually all of the signers of the Declaration of Independence were Freemasons and that, with the exclusion of only three or four individuals, the gathering could have been opened as a Masonic lodge. Actually, out of the 56 signers, we can clearly identify only 8 Freemasons. They are: John Hancock, Benjamin Franklin, William Hooper, William Whipple, Joseph Hewes, Robert Trent Payne, Richard Stockton, and George Walton. Depending on how much inference and supposition one cares to employ, more may be added. Boyden gave the names of 15 whom he regarded as Freemasons; the Masonic Service Association of the Grand Lodge of Iowa named 29; and the Masonic Service Association Of Washington, D. C., has stated that the truth lies somewhere between the two last named figures.

A similar condition exists as to the Delegates to the Constitutional Convention of 1787. Of the 55 Delegates, only 9 signers were Freemasons, 5 other delegates were Freemasons but did not sign, 6 others were not Freemasons at the time but became so later, 13 delegates have been claimed as Freemasons on insufficient evidence, 22 definitely are known not to have been Freemasons.

There were other Masons who rendered valiant service to the cause, though not noted for sighing anything, such as Peyton Randolph, Edmund Randolph, John Pulling Jr., Perez Morton, Robert Livingston, John Cruger, Samuel Kirkland, and others. The list of Masons in military service is a long one and includes some 50 officers. It has been said that Washington's most valued commanders were Freemasons and that he never entrusted an important operation to any other, which is very likely true.

But all patriots were not Freemasons and all Freemasons were not patriots. Out of approximately 100 lodges in the Colonies at the outbreak of hostilities, we know of only one, St. Andrew's Lodge at Boston, which was revolutionary, and that one was extremely so, containing as it did several prominent patriots, Dr. Joseph Warren, Paul Revere, John Hancock, Jonathan W. Edes, Col. Henry Purkett, and John Rowe, the younger, a nephew of John Rowe, Provincial Grand Master of the opposite faction. The sentiment and actions of this one lodge have been used to flavor the whole and give an inaccurate picture of revolutionary sentiment sweeping through the lodges. This lodge met at the Green Dragon Tavern, which was also the meeting place of the "Sons of Liberty" and which was called by Daniel Webster the "Headquarters of the Revolution" but by the British Governor of the Colony, a "nest of sedition." The minutes for one meeting in 1773 state: "Consignees of Tea took up the brethren's time," and for the meeting of December 16, the same year, the Secretary simply covered the page with large scroll capital T's. That was the night of the Boston Tea Party, in which the members of St. Andrew's Lodge participated. On the other hand, the Modern bodies at Boston did not approve such conduct, and in fact had never extended Masonic recognition to St. Andrew's Lodge, which was of Scots registry.

As the War progressed, as Tory sentiment waned, and as patriotism spread through all classes of society, there was a marked erosion of the older or Modern element. The War harmed the Ancients also but left them relatively better off than their rivals, who were rather conclusively discredited by the successful termination of the conflict. John Rowe's Grand Lodge at Boston did not meet during the 12 years from 1775 to 1787, though it may have barely remained alive. At Philadelphia and New York, the Modern bodies simply faded away. By 1785, all of the leading Modern establishments in the Colonies had expired or completely lost momentum. Two new Grand Lodges were erected during the War, Massachusetts in 1777 and Virginia in 1778, the former entirely and the latter partly of Ancient doctrine. When, following the Treaty of Peace, the Craft began to revive and reorganize in other states, there seems to have been no thought of forming other than independent Grand Lodges.

Grand Lodges

Joseph Warren fell while leading the Colonial forces at Bunker Hill, June 17, 1775. On March 8, 1777, the Ancient Provincial Grand Lodge met and elected the Deputy, Joseph Webb, Grand Master, which was more significant than the bare statement might indicate. The rule was that, on the death of a Provincial Grand Master, the office became and remained vacant until filled by appointment of a successor by the Grand Master in Britain. Hence Webb's election was an act of sovereignty and was followed by a circular reciting the circumstances and justifying the procedure, for which it was feared there was little Masonic precedent, though there had been some in the actions of several

German bodies. This first independent Grand Lodge in the United States became known as "Massachusetts Grand Lodge," a name technically to be distinguished from the "Grand Lodge of Massachusetts," later formed. In 1787, John Rowe of the Moderns died and, though his Grand Lodge met in 1790 and 1791, it did not elect his successor. On March 5, 1792, the two Grand Lodges united under the name "The Grand Lodge of the Most Ancient and Honorable Society of Free and Accepted Masons for the Commonwealth of Massachusetts." The second independent Grand Lodge was that of Virginia, formed in 1778. At both Philadelphia and New York, Ancient Masonry gradually superseded the Modern and so overwhelmingly was this true in Pennsylvania that it there became the leading exponent of that doctrine in the United States. It has ever since strictly adhered to the forms, ceremonies, and laws of that branch, even to calling its book of constitutions *Ahiman Rezon*. It so influenced Masonry in Virginia, West Virginia, Maryland, Kentucky, and New York that those jurisdictions are strongly flavored with Ancient doctrine.

Independent Grand Lodges were formed in the thirteen original States as follows: Virginia, 1778; South Carolina, 1783; Pennsylvania, Georgia, and New Jersey, 1786; Maryland, New

York, and North Carolina, 1787; Connecticut, 1789; New Hampshire, 1790; Rhode Island, 1791; Massachusetts, 1792; and Delaware, 1806.

Development of Freemasonry in the United States

The political and economic development of the United States, unique in character, rapidity, and extent, was accompanied by a like unprecedented expansion of Freemasonry. The trek of pioneers across the belt of the Continent can almost be traced by the formation of Masonic lodges and Grand Lodges. During exactly 100 years following the ratification of the Constitution of the United States in 1789, Grand Lodges were formed in 36 additional states and territories (about one-half of them in territories prior to statehood) and in the District of Columbia, making 49 with North Dakota in 1889. Alaska became the 50th in 1981 and Hawaii 51st in 1989.

The Morgan Affair. This growth occurred in spite of a serious anti-Masonic excitement which swept over the eastern, middle western, and, to some extent, the southern states between 1828 and 1840, following the unfortunate "Morgan Affair" at Batavia, New York, in 1826. William

Morgan, supposedly a Freemason but of doubtful standing, having threatened to expose the secrets of the Order, several misguided members of the lodges at Batavia and Canandaigua, later assisted by some as far away as Rochester and Niagara Falls, abducted Morgan, escorted him by horse-drawn carriage across western New York, imprisoned him some days in the old powder magazine at Ft. Niagara, and finally took him across the international boundary and assertedly released him into the custody of Canadian Masons. Since he was never afterwards heard of (though there were unconfirmed reports of him) the Masons were accused of having cast him into the Niagara rapids. Rumors of various kinds spread rapidly through the country; Protestant ministers were foremost in expressing indignation; numerous conventions were assembled to pass resolutions; anti-Masonic tracts and magazines were published and widely circulated. Politicians, discerning the apparent publicity value of the issue, avidly embraced it and eventually formed the "Anti-Masonic Party," which, though it nominated candidates for the Presidency and other offices and had some local successes in several states, died out about 1832. Strangely enough, this party nominated for the presidency William Wirt, a Freemason, and Andrew Jackson, Past Grand

Master of Tennessee, who never wavered in his open loyalty to the Fraternity, was twice elected to the presidency during the period of anti-Masonic excitement. But Freemasonry suffered severely; many lodges, especially in New York and New England, were forced to suspend or surrender their charters; others met only occasionally; and several Grand Lodges were able to hold only token meetings attended by a few officers, thus technically keeping their organizations alive. Like all frenzies, this one died as suddenly as it was born and little was heard of it after 1845.

Masonic Law. To understand the remarkable growth of Freemasonry and the development of Masonic law and jurisprudence in the United States, which has not been emulated elsewhere, we must recall that, in 1787-89, there occurred in this country political events unprecedented in the history of the world, viz., the drafting and ratification of the Constitution of the United States, the rapid settlement and admission of new states, and a great increase in population, commerce, industry, and wealth. There was not only instituted a new, young, and vigorous nation but there was established a condition which set free the energies of men, and, for the first time, there were compiled into a great charter all those ideals of liberty which had slowly developed in the British Isles over many centuries, especially the concept that the powers of government spring from the people and are limited to those delegated by the people. This theory was applied even more fully than it had been in England. There the struggles had been between Parliament and the King, little attempt being made to claim any liberty for the people as against Parliament, the powers of which were and are unlimited. But, under the Constitution of the United States, not only was there a separation and definition of powers between the Congress and the President, but there was a long list of rights of the individual citizen, which was paramount even to the acts of Congress. These were phrased in positive terms; thus, "the writ of habeas corpus shall not be suspended"; "No bill of attainder or ex post facto law shall be passed"; "Congress shall make no law respecting an establishment of religion, or prohibiting the free exercise thereof; or abridging freedom of speech or of the press; or of the right of the people to assemble, and to petition the government for a redress of grievances"; "No soldier shall, in time of peace, be quartered in any house"; "No warrant shall issue, but upon probable cause"; "No person shall be held to answer"; and so on to the number of at least 20 "no's" and "shall not's."

This environment was ideal for Freemasonry. As the restless and energetic people pushed into the forests and plains of the west and south, and on to the Pacific coast, they carried with them political ideas, constitutional maxims, the common law and Freemasonry. Constitutionalism was in the air; every man was conscious of his dignity and individual sovereignty as a citizen and took pride in the sovereignty of his state and nation. The birth of new sovereign states could be witnessed; and the formation of lodges and Grand Lodges, apparently inseparable parts of the same national phenomenon accompanied the erection of counties, municipalities, school districts, and other political institutions.

The old type of General Regulations appropriate to a quiescent Craft, were silent on many practical problems created by a population nervously migrating from one state to another and by the erection of so many new lodges and Grand Lodges. Many questions were presented respecting Masonic regularity and Masonic customs and procedure. Decisions by committees on jurisprudence and by Grand Masters and Grand Lodges were required for which there were no Masonic precedents. Masonic "lawyers" turned to the only other source they knew, their civil laws and constitutions, and they therefore wrote into Masonic law much that came from the political field.

The same local pride and interstate jealousy which had so afflicted the original thirteen states under the Articles of Confederation, only partly mollified by the Federal Constitution, was continued by reason of the wide open spaces and the lack of adequate transportation and communication in the developing domain. The example, set by the original thirteen states by the formation of a Grand Lodge in each seems never to have been questioned as natural and inevitable. Accordingly, each Grand Lodge, like the state in which it was located, became, in Masonic concept, "sovereign," and each became the "peer" of every other Grand Lodge, until Mackey was led to say that societies were but empires in miniature. So, Freemasons had "international" situations to deal with among the many "sovereign" Grand Lodges, and, from the law of nations, they concluded that these relations were governed only by principles of amity and comity.

Soon there developed a body of Masonic "common law," much of which was later incorporated into Grand Lodge constitutions and codes and all of which became the subject matter of no less than 9 works on Masonic law and jurisprudence, published between the years 1856 and 1875.

Prominent among these rules was the "American Doctrine" of exclusive jurisdiction to the effect that there can be but one Grand Lodge in a state and that no Grand Lodge may "invade" the territorial sovereignty of another, though open territory where no such body has been formed any number of Grand Lodges may act. On this principle, a common pattern for the organization of new Grand Lodges was based, whereby, after several lodges, usually three or more, had been established in a state or territory by one or more Grand Lodges, such lodges were competent to form a Grand Lodge of their own. Thereupon, it was deemed, but not without some dissent, that all the lodges in the new state or territory owed allegiance to the new body, irrespective of whether or not they had joined in its organization.

Landmarks. The most notable concept developed by Masonic lawyers and one which created much interest and speculation and not a little furor was the peculiar interpretation they gave to the old term, Landmarks, which had been loosely used in Masonic literature. This term had appeared in the General Regulations adopted by the Grand Lodge at London in 1723 where it was used quite indefinitely. Thereafter it was used by several authors, first in one sense and then in another, without much effort to define what it might include. In America it was received with especial favor and often awe. About the middle of the 19th century Masonic lawyers in this country began to feel that Freemasonry, like a political state, must have a "constitution," consisting of fundamental and indispensable principles, immune from legislative change and to which all Masonic laws, ordinances, edicts, and resolutions must conform. Suddenly, between the years 1856 and 1859, three separate codes of "Ancient Landmarks" appeared in the United States, all different and all supposed to be immemorial and invariable laws and dogma of the Society. The Grand Lodge of Minnesota adopted the first of these in January 1856, its origin being otherwise unknown. In June of the same year, Rob Morris of Kentucky issued one, which bore some resemblance to the first but differed considerably in detail. In 1858 and 1859 Dr. Albert G. Mackey published a third version and made statements indicating that he had not heard of the other two. The idea spread rapidly and a number of Grand Lodges either "adopted" or "accepted" Mackey's list of 25 Landmarks or drew up lists of their own, all differing from each other as well as from the three above mentioned, yet all purporting to be the ancient and immutable laws of the Fraternity. To these were added lists and proposed definitions of landmarks, all variant, until the whole subject was shrouded in disputation and confusion.

The movement met withering blasts from such students as Gould and Pike, but the allurement of the subject was such that, during the following century it was something to be conjured with. In recent years the incongruity has become too apparent to be ignored, so that many have come to regard Landmarks as an impossible problem best to be left alone.

There were seven basic faults in the concept of "Ancient Landmarks." First, although the term "land-marks" had been used in the language and literature of the Society since 1723, it had been but sparingly employed by a few, unmentioned by others, and, when mentioned at all, generally referred to points or features in the ceremonies or lectures. Secondly, the very name, Landmarks, signifies prominent or notorious objects by which other less distinct objects or boundaries can be located, so that, if an object or a proposition does not prove itself but has to he searched for, advocated, or explained, it can be no Landmark in Freemasonry or elsewhere. Thirdly, if Landmarks were unwritten laws, as they were said to be, then, that unwritten character was a part of them and their codification was, in and of itself, a distortion of the law and a destruction of its changeable character. Fourthly, no individual or even Grand

Lodge possessed authority to declare or announce Landmarks or any other fundamental law or doctrine for the whole Fraternity. Fifthly, Landmarks could not be immutable, for no human institution is such. Sixthly, the purported "adoption" or "approval" of Landmarks admitted that they were not fundamental laws binding on all Masons and Masonic bodies, for, if they were, they would have been binding in spite even of an express rejection of them. Lastly, many of the so-called Landmarks did not answer the tests laid down by their proponents; some were not ancient; others originated in written statutory enactments or regulations; and some were mere personal opinions, not even recognized as good Masonic law in many jurisdictions.

Organizations. Nowhere in the world is Freemasonry carried into such extensive application, organization, and diversification as in the United States, where the multiplicity of rites and orders is so great as to be misunderstood, not only by the public, but by a large part of the Fraternity. Besides the well known York and Scottish Rite bodies, there are in the United States no less than 40 orders and organizations of various kinds claiming to be Masonic. In addition, there are national college societies and national clubs composed of Freemasons, and

WILLIAM PRESTON
Author of Monitor and Founder of Modern Ritualistic Instruction

Albert Pike

G∴ Com∴ Supreme Council of 33ᵈ Degree Southern Jurisdiction of U. S.

orders of women, girls, or boys more or less connected with the Fraternity. Practically every kind
of degree practiced anywhere else is available
here, and many that are unknown abroad. The
basic rite is the Craft Rite of the Symbolic Lodges,
which are under the jurisdiction of Grand Lodges,
consisting of the Grand Officers and the Masters
and Wardens of lodges and sometimes Past Masters. With a few exceptions these Grand Lodges
do not recognize as Masonic any degree other than
those of Entered Apprentice, Fellow Craft, and
Master Mason. It is commonly said that, from
Craft or Blue Masonry, two rites, the York Rite
and the Scottish Rite, branch off, but these are
not necessarily coordinate any more than they are
successive stages of instruction. Unfortunately,
Masons in this country have come to regard them
as two separate routes by either of which they may
reach the "Shrine" or "Ancient Arabic Order
Nobles of the Mystic Shrine," although this is not
regarded, and does not regard itself, as Masonic,
except so far as it voluntarily confines its petition-
ers to Knights Templar and 32nd Degree Masons.
Certain degrees of the York Rite bear doctrinal
resemblance to certain degrees of the Scottish
Rite, and, in fact, the Cryptic Degrees were once
side degrees of the latter, but otherwise the degrees of the two systems are in no sense dupli-
cates. Moreover, the different methods of work-

ing in the two Rites are such as to obscure very largely the basic conformity that does exist. While in some foreign countries where Craft lodges have not been opened, the Scottish Rite claims jurisdiction over, and regularly confers the first three degrees, such is not true in the United States and Britain, where a concord exists by which it confines itself to the 4th to the 33rd Degrees.

York Rite

The term, "rite," has come to be used in Freemasonry in a manner somewhat distinct from its basic or original denotation. As so employed, it refers to a group of degrees under the administration of a central body; thus the Capitular Rite includes the degrees of Mark Master, Past Master, Most Excellent Master, and Royal Arch, which are under a Grand Royal Arch Chapter; the Cryptic Rite embraces the degrees of Royal Master and Select Master and an additional ceremony, Super Excellent Master, all under a Grand Council of Royal and Select Masters; and the Templar or Chivalric Rite Consists of the Order of the Red Cross, the Order of Knights of Malta, and the Order of the Temple, which are under a Grand Commandery of Knights Templar. All of these Rites are nationally organized under bodies known, respectively, as the General Grand Chapter of Royal Arch Masons, formed in 1798, the General Grand Council of Royal and Select Masters, formed in 1881, and the Grand Encampment of Knights Templar, formed in 1816. Together, they are commonly called the York Rite, a name derived from the ancient legendary Masonic preeminence of York, England.

Mackey, after exhibiting some uncertainty as to what the York Rite consisted of, finally advocated the substitution of the names "American Rite," which for some years gained considerable favor. But his conclusions were based on suppositions not factually or logically persuasive, such as that the true York Rite had been dismembered by Thomas Dunckerley, who, it was asserted, had transferred the True Word of a Master Mason from the third degree to the Royal Arch. Strange to say, the impossibility of any such transaction did not occur to those who adopted the idea. At the time Dunckerley became influential in Masonry, about 1767, the third degree had been worked in Britain, Europe and America for some years and the Royal Arch had been conferred in Britain and America, so that, not only could these many Masonic bodies not have been led to concur in the change, but even the attempt to put it into execution would have engendered dissention so marked as to be plainly visible at the present day. Moreover, it was not observed that Dunckerley belonged to the Modern branch of the Society and could have had no influence among the Ancients who claimed proprietorship over the Royal Arch and who were caustically critical of virtually everything the Moderns did, basing much of their dissent on slight changes made in the Craft working about 1738 or 39. Mackey's theory was based on the further allegation that a part of the York Rite, the Most Excellent Master's Degree, had been fabricated by Thomas Smith Webb in America, but be did not know, as has later been discovered, that such degree was conferred at Middletown, Connecticut, as early as 1783, when Webb was but a youth.

All of the York Rite Degrees, except the Cryptic, which were once side degrees of the Scottish Rite, are undoubtedly of British origin, though the Royal Arch and Knight Templar ceremonies were probably adaptations from the Cryptic and Chivalric themes originating in France. The inclusion of the Orders of Malta and Knights Templar among Masonic degrees is an apparent anomaly, since they are strongly Christian. So also is the joining in one rite of these degrees with the Order of the Red Cross, which is pagan. The Order of the Temple derives its theme from the Christian knighthood of the Crusades, and many attempts have been made to show a direct descent based on the idea that, upon the dispersion of the Templars and the martyrdom of the Grand Master, Jacques de Molai, 1313-14, the knights found sanctuary among the Freemasons of Scotland and England, some fighting under Robert Bruce at Bannockburn and others erecting the "Baldwin Encampment" at Bristol, England. But the entire absence among the Freemasons of even a legend concerning what would have been an important and startling addition to their ranks, together with the hiatus of some 450 years between the dispersion of the Templars and the earliest record of the modern Order in the latter half of the 18th century, leaves the romances without support.

Strange to say, the earliest preserved minutes of the conferring of the Knight Templar working are those of St. Andrew's Royal Arch Chapter at Boston, Mass., August 28, 1769, the earliest in England being those of Phoenix Lodge No. 257, Portsmouth, for October 21, 1778. Equally strange is the fact that the earliest record of the working of the Royal Arch Degree is in America, the minutes of Fredericksburg Lodge, Virginia, in 1753. At York, England, from 1779, the Royal Arch and Knight Templar Degrees were regularly conferred as the 4th and 5th degrees of the Craft lodge. Several of the York Rite degrees have migrated and, at times, have occupied uncertain places in the schedule of degrees. In England, the Royal Arch has been recognized as Masonic since the Union of 1813, but the Mark Master Degree is not; in Scotland, the Mark is recognized but the Royal Arch is not; in Ireland, both are recognized; while, in the United States, only three or four Grand Lodges recognize either of them.

Scottish Rite

Scottish Rite, the other large group of supplementary degrees, is not, so far as known, Scots either in origin or character, but is French as to both, with some Prussian influence as illustrated by the 21st Degree, Naochite or Prussian Knight, which is evidently of Prussian origin. Indeed, the final 8 degrees were added, supposedly under the Constitutions of 1786, which are claimed to have been validated by Frederick the Great. The perfection and preservation of the present system occurred as if by chance in America, so that the, whole might properly be called the French-Prussian-American Rite. We have observed the great turmoil, which so disturbed continental Masonry, revolving around the Hauts Grades, and the efforts of various bodies to control or to avoid being controlled by them. It was during one of the temporary lulls in the storm, when the Grand Lodge and the Emperors of the East and West, for about a year, were collaborating, that the joint body issued a document, unique in Masonry. It was a patent issued to Etienne (Stephen) Morin in 1761 authorizing him to confer the Rite of Perfection of 25 Degrees in America. He apparently went first to the West Indies where he exercised his prerogatives for a while and then disappeared from the Masonic stage. He passed the Rite along by patents similar to his own, and his patentees carried it into Massachusetts and into New York where a Lodge of Perfection was erected at Albany in 1767. Others set up similar lodges at Philadelphia in 1781 and at Charleston, S. C., in 1783, the latter being destined to become the seat of the Rite, not only in this country, but in the world. By 1797, additional bodies had been established at Baltimore and New York City.

Up to this time, the Rite seems to have been conducted under the French *Constitutions of 1762*, which named only 25 degrees, but somewhat to the bewilderment of later historians, additional *Constitutions of 1786* appeared at Charleston, naming 33 degrees and purporting to be issued under the authority of Frederick the Great. There is no record showing the existence of these later *Constitutions* prior to May 31, 1801, when John Mitchell and Frederick Dalcho, whom Mitchell had deputized only the day before, opened a "Supreme Council of Sovereign

Grand Inspectors General of the 33rd and Last Degree of the Ancient and Accepted Scottish Rite for the United States of America." It is said that the 33rd Degree had been conferred as a detached degree of the Rite of Perfection for several years prior to 1801, though not until the latter date was the term, "Sovereign Grand Inspector General," used.

In 1802, the Charleston Council granted to Count de Grasse-Tilly, son of Admiral de Grasse of the French navy, a patent appointing him Grand Commander for the French Antilles and authorizing him to erect and inspect lodges, Councils and consistories in both East and West Hemispheres. Intending to return to St. Domingo, de Grasse-Tilly was diverted by the renewal of the revolt there and went to Paris instead, where he arrived in 1804 and where he established a Supreme Council, which soon became embroiled in the discord plaguing French Masonry previously described. But his activities were not confined to France, for between 1807 and 1810 he erected Councils in St. Domingo and Jamaica and, from one or both these sources, his Rite naturally found its way into Louisiana where it was enthusiastically received by the predominantly French population. Following this example, the Grand Orient of France also established bodies of the Rite in

Louisiana, thereby, transmitting into that State the theory of Scottish Rite jurisdiction over Craft Degrees, which had done so much harm in France. It created discord in Louisiana Masonry for many years, and, upon the appeal for aid made by the Grand Lodge of that State to the other Grand Lodges, more than half of them severed fraternal relations with the Grand Orient.

Notwithstanding that Dr. Albert G. Mackey was Secretary General of the Scottish Rite bodies at Charleston, Albert Pike, admitted in 1853, became their most valuable member. Almost at once, he began the arduous task of revising the rituals of the Rite, which, according to his statements, he found in a chaotic and incoherent condition. His intellect being appreciated, he was elected Grand Commander in 1859 and held that office until his death in 1891. An indefatigable student, a lawyer, and a prolific writer, he perfected the organization of the Southern Supreme Council, rationalized the constitutional basis of the Rite, advised with and helped to subdue schisms in the Northern Council, rewrote the rituals, and, in addition to numerous tracts and addresses, compiled *Morals and Dogma,* the last named being the product of some ten years of exploration in ancient religions, philosophies, mysteries, and societies, which he conceived to be the forerunners of

Freemasonry and by which he explained the doctrine, ceremonies, and symbolism of the Rite.

Although the Scottish Rite had been first introduced into the northern states and had spread somewhat extensively there by the turn of the 19th century, it was not until after the Civil War that a condition of harmony and stability was realized north of the Mason and Dixon Line. In 1806, Antoine Bideaud and Joseph Cerneau separately arrived in New York City with the purpose of disseminating Scottish Masonry. The former was a member of de Grasse-Tilly's Supreme Council in St. Domingo but apparently had no authority to operate in the United States. The latter possessed only the 25 degrees of the Rite of Perfection and, as to those, had authority only in Cuba. Undaunted by any such limitations, Cerneau proceeded in 1807 to open a Consistory of the 32nd Degree in New York, and, in 1813, erected a Supreme Council in New Orleans, claiming jurisdiction over the Craft Degrees. By the latter year, such serious conflict had arisen between the Bideaud and Cerneau bodies in the North that Inspector General de la Motta of the Charleston Council was moved to investigate their respective claims. He recognized the Bideaud Council and pronounced the Cerneau bodies spurious, whereupon the latter retaliated by establishing a Council of Princes of Jerusalem at

Charleston. In 1827 Cerneau departed for France and was no longer heard of, but his various lodges, chapters, and councils continued to exist and cause dissention until the reconciliation of 1867.

Until the latter date, Scottish Masonry in the North was of such protean character that the ramifications of its many factions are difficult to follow, and there is little doubt that many Masons of good intentions were inveigled into spurious bodies in ignorance of any clear understanding of what was regular and what was irregular. The succession of councils was somewhat as follows: In 1832, Count de St. Laurent's "Supreme Council 33rd Degree for Terra Firma, South America, New Spain, Canary Islands, Puerto Rico" etc. and his "United Supreme Council for the Western Hemisphere," for brevity called the "Hicks Body"; In 1848, Henry C. Atwood's "Supreme Council for the United States"; In 1851, the "Cross Body" or "Supreme Council 33rd Degree for the United States of America"; In 1852, the second "Atwood Body"; In 1860, the "Hays Body" or "Supreme Council for the North Masonic Jurisdiction of the Western Hemisphere." In 1844 the old Bideaud Council revived from the anti-Masonic crusade and two years later instituted the first Scottish Rite Council in England. By 1858 it had 43 subordinate lodges, chapters, and councils in 9 of the 14 northern states over which it claimed jurisdiction, but suddenly experienced a schism which split it into two factions, one headed by K. H. Van Rensselaer and the other by Edward A. Raymond. In 1863 the Hays Body at New York merged with the Raymond Body at Boston, forming the "Supreme Council for the Northern Jurisdiction of the United States." Meanwhile Albert Pike and a committee from the southern Supreme Council, which had been investigating conditions in the north, concluded that both the Van Rensselaer and Raymond Councils were illegal and recommended that they consolidate. That was accomplished May 15, 1867, since which time the career of Scottish Masonry in the North has been peaceful and prosperous, though some trouble was made in 1872 by Henry J. Seymour and in 1881 by Hopkins Thompson, both of whom attempted to create rival councils, without permanent success.

Though claims were made at times by various Scottish Rite Supreme Councils in the North of right to establish and govern Craft lodges conferring the three degrees, the united opposition of the Grand Lodges made this such a dangerous position for bodies whose very right to exist at all was in question that the rival bodies not only relinquished the claim, but sought favor by attributing such claim to their rivals. For many years now the exclusive jurisdiction of the Grand Lodges over Craft Masonry has been fully recognized by all bodies of every kind in this country. By like conciliation, the territorial division between the Northern and Southern Councils, though not definitely settled for some years, was finally agreed upon as the Ohio River and the Mason and Dixon Line, Delaware being conceded to the North. The Northern Jurisdiction has exclusive jurisdiction in, and is limited to, the States of Maine, New Hampshire, Vermont, Massachusetts, Connecticut, Rhode Island, New York, New Jersey, Pennsylvania, Delaware, Ohio, Indiana, Illinois, Michigan, and Wisconsin. The Southern Jurisdiction, with headquarters now at Washington, D. C., has jurisdiction over the rest of the world, except so far as it has surrendered it to Supreme Councils in various countries.

CHAPTER VIII

Freemasonry in Relation to Other Societies

Freemasonry and Ancient Paganism

ROBABLY THE MOST curious aspect of Masonic literature is the abundance of theories about the supposed descent of Freemasonry from ancient paganism, ancient mysteries, magism, and other oriental cults and philosophies. How did any such idea come to be imposed upon a society which plainly grew out of a fraternity of stonemasons, architects and builders, who, so far as we know, had no interest in such things and probably would have been excommunicated by the Church for heresy or blasphemy if they had displayed any such tendency? There is nothing in the Gothic Legends or Charges remotely bearing upon the subject.

From 1598, we have minutes of various lodges in Scotland but they contain nothing about it. Nor do the writings of Ashmole, Plot, Aubrey, Holme, or any other author of the 17th century in England.

Dr. James Anderson prefaced his *Constitutions of 1723* with a fabulous history of Masonry, thereby displaying a very lively imagination, but he gave no hint of any mystical or magical origin of the Craft. The first mention of the subject in connection with Masonry is to be found in the diary of Dr. Wm. Stukeley, a London physician and divine, who tells us that he was made a Mason in London in 1721 and that his curiosity had led him to enter the Fraternity, suspecting it to be the remains of the Mysteries of the ancients. From the nature of the statement, it seems that he did not find what he was looking for.

Beginning in 1723 and continuing for many years a number of different versions of what pretended to be Masonic rituals were exposed by publication. These indicated a variety of ceremonies practiced by the various lodges, but there was nothing in them savoring of ancient mysteries or paganism.

In 1730 and 1737, two of the most consequential statements ever made concerning Freemasonry were voiced, the first in England, the second in France. The former was contained in the

Defense of Masonry by Martin Clare in answer to Samuel Prichard's *Masonry Dissected,* which had charged that Freemasonry was "nothing but an unintelligible heap of stuff and jargon, without common sense or connection," "a ridiculous imposition," and "pernicious." In answer, Clare said in part:

"Considering through what obscurity and darkness this mystery has been delivered down, the many centuries it has survived, the many countries and languages and sects and parties it has run through, we are rather to wonder it ever arrived at the present age without more imperfections. In short, I am apt to think that Masonry, as it is now explained, has in some circumstances declined from its original purity. It has run long in muddy streams, and, as it were, underground; but notwithstanding the great rust it may have contracted, and the forbidding light in which it is placed by the dissector, there is still much of the old fabric remaining; the essential pillars of the building may be discovered through the rubbish, though the superstructure be overrun with moss and ivy, and the stones, by length of time, be disjointed."

He proceeded to refer to the Egyptian practice of concealing mysteries in hieroglyphics, the possible descent of Masonry from the Pythagorean and the similarity of Masonry to the discipline, of the Essenes, the Cabalists, the Druids, and other ancient sects.

Seven years later the Chevalier Ramsay, in a charge to some candidates in a lodge at Paris, expressed the Principal theme that Freemasonry was not the outgrowth of an architectural fraternity, but of the Chivalric Crusaders and that the Knights and Princes, on their return from the last Crusade, had established bodies of the Order throughout western Europe. He included a short subsidiary statement, somewhat inconsistent with his main theme, as follows:

"Yes, Sirs, the famous festivals of Ceres at Eleusis, of Isis in Egypt, of Minerva at Athens, or Urania amongst the Phoenicians, and of Diana in Scythia were connected with ours. In those places mysteries were celebrated which concealed many vestiges of the ancient religion of Noah and the Patriarchs."

The chivalric, knightly, or noble origin of Freemasonry took hold immediately and resulted in the fabrication of numerous Hauts Grades, which practically dominated Freemasonry in France, Germany, and other Countries on the Continent for a century or more, and a small remnant of which are now preserved in the Scottish Rite.

But the ancient mystery doctrine voiced by Clare and Ramsay was very slow in arousing interest, not a single book or address in England for many years taking any note of it. Neither Calcott, Preston, nor any other English writer mentioned the subject, except Hutchinson, who briefly adverted to it in 1775. The idea seems first to have been taken up by the Abbe Robin in France in *Researches in Ancient and Modern Initiations* (1779), followed by J. S. Vogel in *Letters Concerning Freemasonry (1785),* and Osnabruck in Germany (1789). The first thorough presentation was made by Alexander Lenoir in *Freemasonry Traced to its True Origin,* or *The Antiquity of Freemasonry Proved by the Explication of Ancient* and *Modern Mysteries (1814).* From that time the theory spread rapidly and attained great popularity, many books being published on the subject and many speakers and writers accepting it without question.

This occurred during the period when it was commonly believed that Freemasonry had originated in the East many centuries ago, at least as early as the building of King Solomon's Temple (1000 BC) but possibly earlier. Accordingly, it was quite consistent with prevailing views. But it was not accepted by those who had begun the study of the history of Freemasonry by the only proper method, that of examining the records of society itself. Neither Findel, the great German historian, nor Lyon in Scotland, nor Rebold in France, nor Gould and Hughan in England, accepted the theory. But, before the work of the realistic school (1865-1885) had established the falsity of the notions on which the theory was largely based, it had become fixed in Masonic literature.

Mackey and Pike entered the Fraternity in the 1840's when this type of writing was rising to its culmination, and neither of them seems to have questioned it in the slightest degree. Dr. Mackey, in his *Ritualist* (1867), and *Symbolism* (1869), went to revolting extremes, making out that practically everything in Masonry and every piece of furniture in the lodge were some remnants of Pagan sun-worship or sex-worship and reducing God to an hermaphrodite, he-she being; the columns were said to be relics of phallic or sex-worship and represented the male generative organs; the circle was the cteis or female organ. (*Ritualist,* p. 61 et seq.). Then, by taking the tetragrammaton, JHV H, and turning it around, Mackey obtained H V H J, saying that V was pronounced like the vowel 0 and J was pronounced like the vowel I. Thus, he produced Ho-Hi, which he said meant in Hebrew He-She, representing the bisexual character of God. (*Symbolism*, p. 185 et seq.). Yet, he told us later in his *Encyclopaedia* (1874), under the title, Jehovah, that the Hebrew had no vowel sounds but that these had to be supplied by the reader. In justice to Mackey, it is necessary to say that he finally joined the factual school and became more sensible to reality, saying in his

History (published posthumously in 1896) at p. 185:

"It has been a favorite theory with several German, French, and British scholars to trace the origin of Freemasonry to the Mysteries of Paganism, while others, repudiating the idea that the modern association should have sprung from them, still find analogies so remarkable between the two systems as to lead them to suppose that the Mysteries were an offshoot from the Pure Freemasonry of the Patriarchs.

"In my opinion there is not the slightest foundation in historical evidence to support either theory, although I admit the existence of many analogies between the two systems, which can, however, be easily explained without admitting any connection in the way of origin and descent between them."

and at p. 197:

"For myself, I can only arrive at what I think is a logical conclusion; that if both the Mysteries and Freemasonry have taught the same lessons by the same methods of instruction, this has arisen not from a succession of organization, each one a link in a long chain of historical sequences leading directly to another, until Hiram is simply substituted for Osiris, but rather from those usual and natural coincidences of human thought which are to be found in every age and among all people.

"It is, however, hardly to be denied that the founders of the Speculative system of Masonry, in forming their ritual, especially of the third degree, derived suggestions as to the form and character of their funeral legend from the rites of the ancient initiations."

[**182**]

Albert Pike probably never entertained the slightest doubt that Freemasonry was derived from the ancient religions and philosophies, though he was a more profound student than was Mackey. He denied that the Kabalah, the Sohar, or any commentary thereon, attributed sexual or bisexual character to Deity, but on the contrary averred that Deity was depicted as infinite, unknowable, and without any conformation whatever. *(Morals and Dogma,* p. 765.) He did insist that Freemasonry was an inheritance from ancient paganism and this theory is expressed throughout *Morals and Dogma*, which he completed about 1872. Accordingly, he had no patience with what he considered the puerilities of Blue Masonry, saying (*id.* p. 819):

"The blue degrees are but the outer court and portico of the Temple. Part of the symbols are displayed there to the Initiate, but he is intentionally misled by false interpretations. It is not intended that he should understand them; but it is intended that he shall imagine that he understands them."

He did not answer the common sense question of why any one in formulating symbolic Masonry would want to incorporate hidden meanings, which no one would understand, and furthermore, imagining that one understood them, no other meanings would be sought. That scheme would seem to have been wholly without purpose.

It is quite common for savants to write extensively about the secrets of the ancients and the extreme precautions taken to hide them from the masses of people or even from posterity. Then they either neglect to inform us what those secrets were or, attempting to do so, supply only some trite explanation, which amounts to an anticlimax. Frequently this proves to be nothing more than the supposed Ineffable Name of Deity, which a moment's reflection would tell us is illusory and immaterial, for, if Deity be an omnipotent, omniscient, and omnipresent Spiritual Being, no name that man could express in words or letters would adequately describe Him or indicate His attributes.

What has been said about the relation of the ancient mysteries to Freemasonry applies as well to Rosicrucianism, Druidism, Culdeeism, and other sects which fertile imaginations have employed to explain the origin or character of Freemasonry. The important fact is that no Grand Lodge has ever adopted any such theory, and the whole idea is non-Masonic so far as official doctrine goes. Freemasonry is no more occult than the Golden Rule; no more mysterious than Morality.

It is fitting to close this discussion with the opinion of one of the Fraternity's greatest antiquaries, William J. Hughan, who, in his article in the *Encyclopaedia Britannica* (11th Ed.), deemed it useless to investigate

"still older societies which may have been utilized and imitated by the Fraternity, but which in no sense can be accepted as the actual forebearers of the present society of Free and Accepted Masons. They were the predecessors, possibly prototypes, but not near relations or progenitors of the Freemasons."

Freemasonry and Religion

Freemasonry is not a religion. Nothing in Ancient craft masonry characterizes it as such. It has no creed, no dogma, and no theology. It saves no souls and it does not compete with any organized religion. It accepts good men regardless of their religious beliefs in an effort to make them better men.

Just as the members of a denomination, or sect, may not have exactly the same concept of its creed, so Masons may differ in their understanding of Freemasonry. They do, however, in concert, perform certain religious demonstrations formalized in the ritual, manifesting belief in a spiritual power on whom the Mason is dependent and to whom he is responsible.

Freemasonry has been attacked on two fronts - political and religious by bigots who see the Fraternity as a competitor and rival for time, energy, and money of their adherents. One group, the Christian Ministries, criticizes and say Freemasonry is not compatible with Christianity and that Masons are therefore "unbelievers." Anti-Masonic critics are, in most cases critics because the Masons are non-members of the critics' own particular group. But there are thousands of different religious sects, each expounding that they have "the truth."

Freemasonry promotes the right of the individual to think for himself and to make his own choices.

It should be remembered that in the early 1700s practically the only writers were the Catholic scriveners, or monks, who were accustomed to beginning, ending and interspersing religious phrases in all documents - a practice carried out even today in many documents which are not religious. We find many such phrases in Masonic documents.

Freemasonry came into being out of the craft and science of the builders as well as from the deep divinely given instincts of man to rise above the material and to deal with the mystical and spiritual portion of existence.

Freemasonry and religion are linked by the factors of their heritage and the nature of man. All Masons believe in the Deity without reservation. However, Masonry makes no demands as to how a member thinks of the Great Architect. Freemasonry is a supplement to good living with faith in God. It is supportive of morality and virtue. It teaches that it is important for every man to have a religion of his own and to be faithful to it through thought and action.

It is very likely that Masonry was not intended in its beginning to be religious. It was basically architectural or scientific, though the ancient Charges almost invariably began with a Trinitarian invocation and charged the Masons to be "true men of God and Holy Church." In the exposes of the ritual, which began to be published in 1723, we find religious symbolism. For example in the *Grand Mystery of Free-Masons Discover'd* we find:

"What Lodge are you of? The Lodge of St. John.
"How many lights? Three: a Right East, South and West.
"What do they represent? The Three Persons, Father, Son and Holy Ghost.
"How many Pillars? Two, Iachin and Boaz.
"What do they represent? A Strength and Stability of the Church in all Ages."

The Grand Lodge of 1717 seems to have submerged the religious motif and employed more the architectural or scientific. Charge I, as adopted in 1723, was entitled, "Concerning God and Religion," but the name of God does not appear in the text of that or any other Charge.

Charge I reads as follows:

"CONCERNING GOD AND RELIGION.

"A Mason is oblig'd by his Tenure, to obey the moral Law; and if he rightly understands the Art, he will never be a stupid Atheist, nor an irreligious Libertine. But though in ancient Times Masons were charg'd in every Country to be of the Religion of that Country or Nation, whatever it was, yet 'tis now thought more expedient to oblige them to that Religion in which all Men agree, leaving their particular Opinions to themselves: that is, to be good Men and true, or Men of Honor and Honesty, by whatever Denominations or Persuasions they may be distinguish'd; whereby Masonry becomes the Center of Union, and the Means of conciliating true Friendship among Persons that must have remain'd at a perpetual Distance."

This did not mean that the founders of the Grand Lodge were irreligious, for two of the principal actors, Desaguliers and Anderson, were Christian ministers. It merely means that they did not view the Society as a religious body, but rather chose to leave that matter to the church. On the other hand, the Grand Lodge regularly held its Annual Communications on St. John the Baptist's Day and one of its Quarterly Communications on St. John the Evangelist's Day. In a Christian nation, especially one having an established church, it is hardly to be expected that religion can be excluded from a society inculcating morality as Masonry did. Accordingly, we find that of some

22 Masonic addresses delivered between 1730 and 1787, 16 mention reverence for God and 6 are silent on the subject; 5 refer to immortality of the soul and 17 do not; 8 contain Christian doctrine while 14 do not; and none of them indicates that any religious requirement was made of the candidate. This suggests that there was a period of about fifty years during which there seems to have been considerable doubt as to the religious content of Freemasonry. Toward the end of that period, in 1772, William Preston became very influential by reason of his lectures and his authorship of *Illustrations of Masonry.* He definitely promoted the religious movement in the Society, saying, among other things:

"Religion is the only tie which can bind men, and that where there is no religion, there can be no Masonry ... Hence the doctrine of a God, the creator and preserver of the universe, has been their firm belief in every age."

He was, however, vague as to whether the doctrine of the Craft was Christian, averring that, where it was the religion of a country, Masons acquiesced in it, and his whole discussion was rhetorical rather than specific. The statement, repeated many times, that Preston persuaded the Grand Lodge in 1760 to adopt the Bible as a Great Light is false, for he was not then a Mason, and, after becoming such in 1762 or 63, he did not for some years attain suf-

[189]

ficient influence to accomplish any such purpose.

William Hutchinson, in 1775, with the approval of the officers of the Grand Lodge, published his *Spirit of Masonry,* the first book to present the philosophical aspect of Freemasonry. His theme was that Masonry and Christianity had both developed out of the patriarchal religion and that the Society, in its "third stage," was of Christian faith.

In America, Webb's *Monitor*, first published in 1797, contained this statement:

"and the Blazing Star, in the center, is commemorative of the star which appeared to guide the wise men of the East to the place of our Saviour's nativity."

That clause was disapproved by the Baltimore Convention of 1843 but remained in reprints of the Monitor as late as 1869.

Dr. George Oliver, one of the most productive of Masonic writers, who published some two dozen Masonic books over a period of about forty years, positively and repeatedly insisted that the doctrine of Masonry was Christian. This theme is particularly evident in his *Symbol of Glory* (1850) and *The Revelations of a Square* (1855).

So for some years the issue seemed to be whether Masonry was Christian or merely monotheistic. The three Grand Lodges of Prussia and those of Norway, Sweden, and Denmark have always been Christian. At the Union of 1813 between the two Grand Lodges of England, all Christian references were stricken from the ritual and provision was made for the dedication of lodges to Moses and Solomon instead of the two Saints John. In 1815, Charge I of 1723 was amended to require the candidate to "believe in the glorious architect of heaven and earth and practice the sacred duties of morality."

The Grand Orient of France, in 1849, departed from the English position of that time by amending its constitution to provide that "Freemasonry has for its principles the existence of Deity and the immortality of the soul." In 1877 this was again amended to read: "Masonry has for its principles mutual tolerance, respect for others and for itself, and absolute liberty of conscience." Two years later the Grand Orient made the display of the Bible optional with the lodges. This aroused some resentment in England and America, though it is not true, as so often stated, that it caused many American Grand Lodges to sever fraternal relations with the Grand Orient, for the reason that most of them had done so some years previously for an entirely different cause, the invasion of American jurisdictions.

God. Masonic authorities give different interpretations of the Deity. Mackey said that the candidate must believe in "God or the Great Architect of the Universe." Some jurisdictions in this country require belief in a "Supreme Being or T.G.A.O.T.U."; "God the Father"; "a Supreme Being"; "God, the Creator, Author, and Architect of the Universe, Omnipotent, Omniscient, and Omnipresent" and merely "Monotheism."

Immortality. Mackey said that belief in immortality was included in the requirements simply as subsidiary to belief in God, meaning apparently that one who believes in God must believe in immortality, but that is not necessarily so. There is considerable difference among Masonic authorities on the subject of a future life. Some are satisfied with mere immortality of the soul but others require "Resurrection to a Future Life" or "Resurrection of the Body."

V.S.L. The relation of the Bible to Freemasonry is treated in a variety of ways, and even the ritual is not clear on this point, for it is there referred to both as a part of the furniture of the lodge and also as one of the Great Lights. The Bible was first referred to as a part of the furniture of the lodge about 1730. A little later we find the Bible, Square, and Compasses described as Pillars of the Lodge. The first known reference to Great Lights is found in France in 1745 but this meant what are now called the Lesser Lights. The Ancient Grand Lodge of England made the first use of the Bible, Square, and Compasses as the Three Great Lights in 1760, which example was followed by the Moderns in 1762. While Preston's *Illustrations of Masonry* did not call the Bible part of the furniture, his lectures seemed to indicate that it was, but Preston never referred to the Bible, Square, and Compasses as the Three Great Lights. In 1929 representatives of the Grand Lodges of England, Ireland, and Scotland agreed that the Great Lights consisted of the Volume of Sacred Law, Square, and Compasses, though, in 1938, they seemed to consider the Bible and Volume of Sacred Law the same thing. Often the Bible is called "the Great Light," thus separating it from and elevating it above the Square and Compasses.

If the Bible is the Great Light in Masonry, obviously many Freemasons in the world do not have Masonic light and the universality of Masonry is destroyed. To avoid this dilemma, some say that, in countries where other religions prevail, the Koran, the Rig Veda, or some other sacred writings may be supplied. But no one has gone so far as to say that such other books are

Great Lights even in those other lands. The better view would seem to be that some Volume of Sacred Law is necessary in the lodge as a symbol of Divine revelation, but without any requirement that it be believed or constitute a Great Light.

It is difficult to see how the Bible can be the Great Light of Masonry unless Masons believe its contents. But Jews do not believe the New Testament and many Christians do not accept most of the Old. If Masonry is non-Christian, how can the New Testament shed light upon it? Mackey said that the V. S. L. should be that which by the religion of the country was believed to contain the revealed word of the Great Architect. What is meant by the "religion of the country" where a number of diverse religions are believed? Does it mean that the majority rules and that the minorities must be satisfied with what they do not accept as revealed word?

The various concepts of a Supreme Being, a Future Life, and a V. S. L. may be arranged in many combinations, and, hence, the official doctrines of the many Grand Lodges present danger of discord if their relative merits are debated. Perhaps it would be best not to discuss such matters with too great particularity, but enthusiastic and careless writers keep the issue alive by urging their several religious concepts.

Freemasonry and Roman Catholicism

Does Freemasonry exclude Roman Catholics? No. There have been and still are Catholic Freemasons. Viscount Montague, a Catholic, was Grand Master of England in 1732. Lord Petre, a leader among English Catholics, was Grand Master from 1772 to 1777 and thereafter attended Grand Lodge for many years. In 1874, Lord Ripon, Grand Master of England, resigned for the stated reason that he had been converted to the Catholic faith and deemed his religion incompatible with Freemasonry, but this came as a surprise to the Fraternity. John Hoban, the architect in charge of the construction of the Capitol and the White House in Washington, D.C., and one of the charter members of Federal Lodge No. 15 of the District of Columbia was a Catholic, as were some of his associates in that Lodge. Albert Pike stated that, in Latin-American countries, there were over 100,000 Catholic members of the Scottish Rite.

The truth is that Freemasonry has been out of bounds for communicants of the Church of

Rome for more than two centuries, ever since the Bull, *In Eminenti,* of Pope Clement XII, promulgated in 1738. Eight Popes have issued no less than seventeen Bulls or Encyclicals denouncing Freemasonry and forbidding Catholics to join the Order, the latest being that of Pope Leo XIII in 1902, but the most notorious being *Humanum Genus* by the same author in 1884.

It is a common error to suppose that the estrangement arises from inconsistency between the secrecy of Freemasonry and the disclosures implicit in the confessional. Whether or not such inconsistency exists would seem to be trivial in view of the positive, severe, and oft repeated castigation of the Fraternity by the Church. Moreover, it is not alone Freemasonry or even secret societies that have come under Papal denunciation. As late as 1950, the Pope denounced Rotary International and inferentially all other so-called service clubs, which are usually deemed harmless, if not beneficent by the public. One of the most presumptuous Papal Encyclicals was that, which about the same year, instructed Catholic judges in the United States to refuse to enter decrees for divorce, thus purporting to interfere with the administration of the civil laws of the country. It would seem that he might properly have demanded that they resign their positions rather than enter decrees of divorce; but he did not say that but contemplated that, retaining their offices, they would give precedence to Church law over the civil law.

Upon reflection, one need not wonder at these odd manifestations of assumed power. Catholicism is not, according to its doctrine, merely a religion or one of the religions but the only true religion; all others are heretical and evil, indeed no religions at all. The Church does not regard the St. James version or the Revised version as Bibles; only the Vulgate is such, though the ordinary person would scarcely observe any difference between them. Moreover, the Catholic Church does not attach the same weight to the Bible as do Protestant denominations. Catholic doctrine seems to be that the Scriptures are not the only revelation but only part of the revelation of God's will or law, and that other and quite as important revelations may come from time to time through the Pope, who is supposed to be God's Vicar on earth.

The Church of Rome or the Vatican is, in theory at least, a political state. It did formerly exercise ordinary political sovereignty and monarchial powers over a broad territory which it did not have the military strength to retain. Yet the Vatican, now restricted to about 100 acres in the city of Rome, has a flag, coins money, sends and receives ambassadors, indulges in political intrigue, and assumes the prerogatives of a sovereign state. In political theory, the Church is and always has been monarchial and anti-republican. Kings were and are, in its view, rulers by Divine right, symbolically represented by the coronation of the prince by the Pope or an archbishop.

Education recognized by the Church is that accompanied by religious indoctrination, the questionable element of which is that the religion may dominate or distort the scientific or factual phases. The American doctrine of the separation of Church and State is to Catholicism an abomination.

The supposed prejudice which Freemasons hold against the Church of Rome is simply a distrust of the machinations of that Church-State and is no more marked than it is among the American public at large. In neither is it a religious prejudice, as clearly shown by the fact that several other sects are not distrusted, though they are quite as formalized, for example, the various Lutheran denominations and the "high" Episcopal Church, and some may be called queer, such as the Friends or Quakers.

The American people, Freemasons among them, do not want their civil servants and political officials to receive instructions or even advice from Rome or any other foreign center.

Freemasonry believes in freedom of religion, separation of Church and State, secular education, and republican government. American citizens who are Roman Catholic must disagree with the outmoded political notions of the Pope and take with a grain of salt much that appears in the Church's *Bulls* and *Encyclicals*. In 1928, Albert E. Smith, a Catholic and former governor of New York State, ran for President on the Democratic ticket and was defeated by Herbert Hoover largely on the religious issue. But, in 1960, John Fitzgerald Kennedy, a Catholic running on the Democratic ticket was elected President of the U.S. He proved to be a patriotic, a much loved and admired President and the country suffered no obvious Papal interference.

If there is any clash between the Church and Freemasonry, the former is the aggressor, for no Grand Lodge has ever paid the slightest heed to any of those repeated attacks, though Albert Pike, when Grand Commander of the Scottish Rite, issued a devastating reply and analysis of *Humanum Genus* in 1884. In justification it must be observed that the Scottish Rite is more widely dispersed than York or Blue Masonry and, in many Catholic countries, is the principal if not the only Freemasonry. It has there had ample reason to fear and resist the efforts at Papal domination.

Nation after nation has been forced to repudiate the Catholic See and those which did so became leaders in political freedom, scientific advancement, industry, commerce, learning, and social development. No Catholic country has been able to retain more than a remnant of its former glory. In the New World where all had an even chance, Catholic countries have lagged far behind Protestant countries in every respect.

Freemasonry does not oppose the Catholic Church or any church. With all its faults, that Church has done much good; it has faithfully stood by its religious creed, often in the face of popular clamor. If its dogma contains pretensions or error, it also contains much that is good. It, at least, wears the jewel of consistency and does not compromise with deviations as a matter of expediency. There is too much evil in the world to justify strife between those who stand for the right. So far as the Catholic Church teaches cardinal virtues and spreads the ameliorating influence of religion, it will enjoy the complete confidence of Freemasons, but if the Church would do only that, it would never imagine anything wrong about Freemasonry.

Freemasonry and Mormonism

Conflicting and sometimes erroneous statements have appeared in printed books and articles on this subject. In 1972, Melvin B. Hogan, a Past Master, Past Grand Orator and Grand Chaplain of the Grand Lodge of Utah, as well as Secretary of the Grand Lodge of Research of Utah, was uniquely granted privileged access to the primary resources within the Historical Archives of the Mormon Church in Salt Lake City. His research resulted in a careful and comprehensive perspective of this historical period which appears in Vol. 2 of the *Little Masonic Library* (1977 rev. ed.) It is an unbiased account and the author has gone to considerable detail to bolster his statements where he gives his own opinion.

Historical accounts dealing with the introduction of Freemasonry among the Mormons in the "Illinois episode" have been intentionally omitted and distorted by both the Masons and the Mormons from mid 1841 to 1976. The country was young, the Mormon Church, founded in 1830, was struggling to sustain itself in the wake of the "Morgan Affair" and the anti-Masonic turmoil when they made their exit to Nauvoo, Ill. in 1842. Passions ran high. There was fault on both sides.

Joseph Smith, together with his older brother Hyrum (who was a member of Mt.

Moriah Lodge No. 112, Palmyra, N.Y.), Samuel Harrison Smith, Oliver Cowdery, David Whitmer and Peter Whitmer, Jr., on April 6, 1830, at Fayette, N.Y., organized what is identified as the Church of Jesus Christ of Latter-day Saints, or more commonly known, the Mormon Church. Joseph Smith is claimed as their Prophet.

The Church has built its theology and dogma on four volumes of sacred scripture, namely: The *Holy Bible* (KJV), *The Book of Mormon, Doctrine and Covenants*, and *The Pearl of Great Price*. The Articles of Faith are found in the last named. In studying this, it is difficult to find conflicts or incompatibilities between the teachings of Mormonism and the philosophy, principles, and tenets of Freemasonry. If anything, the Mormons seem to require greater adherence to principles of morality and right living than do the Freemasons. Few sects or classes are better qualified than the Mormons for Masonic application for, as a group, they are prudent, conscientious and demand exemplary behavior from their members.

What was the Masonic situation in Nauvoo, Illinois in 1842? The Grand Master was Abraham Jonas, a complex and colorful individual, and the Grand Lodge engaged in some unusual transactions with the Mormons. On March 5, 1842 Jonas personally instituted a lodge at Nauvoo and made Joseph Smith a Mason-at-Sight. It was only natural that other members who had followed their founder from N.Y. would also petition the lodge and of which Hyrum Smith was Master. Politics played a part too. Jonas was seeking election to the state legislature. He constituted lodges which were practically 100% of Mormon membership and these Jonas lodges attracted other Mormons who were a clannish group to begin with. Neighboring lodges objected on several grounds: one because the petitioner was from an out of state lodge which had rejected him. Also, the neighboring lodges were not pleased with the Mormons taking over by virtue of their majority. The history and purposes of the lodge at Nauvoo were in all things subordinate to influence emanating from the Mormon center. Nearly all members of the Mormon Hierarchy joined. The neighboring lodges also accused the Mormons of appropriating Masonic symbols and practices. But it should be remembered that most symbols have a universal and common heritage and from ancient days have been adopted by many cultures. Likewise, principles of morality do not belong to any one ethnic group but are universal and demanding of many different adherents.

Dispensations were granted, objected to, withdrawn, and reinstated again. In 1843, the Grand Lodge ordered the Mormon lodges to be dissolved and to cease Masonic labor. They re-

fused. A bitter feud between the Smith brothers with the Church on one side and with neighboring lodges, who were antagonistic, climaxed
in 1844 with the murder of the Smith brothers
in the Carthage jail on June 27, 1844 by a mob
and the removal of the whole Mormon community from Illinois to the far West under the leadership of Brigham Young.

Following the murder of Joseph and Hyrum
Smith, Brigham Young, a staunch Freemason,
judiciously introduced the inflexible policy that
the Mormon Church had nothing to say pub-
licly regarding Freemasonry and, thenceforth,
would make no statement relating to the Order
under any circumstance. Young took his Masonry, as well as his Church, seriously and believed that nothing constructive could result
from continuing exchanges over the years from
the Mormon Church and Freemasonry.

The first five Presidents of the Mormon
Church were Freemasons: Joseph Smith, the
Prophet, Brigham Young, John Taylor, Wilford
Woodruff and Lorenzo Snow. They were all
made Masons in Nauvoo Lodge. During
Nauvoo's existence almost 1500 men became
members of the Lodge.

The Grand Lodge of Illinois, formed in 1840,
suffered a fire in 1852 and lost valuable documents and records. These would have been rich

in material. Besides the loss by fire, many of the actual vital details were deliberately never recorded and doubtless never will be, although some Nauvoo records are in the Archives of the Mormon Church.

The Mormon Community entered Utah on July 24, 1847 under the able leadership of Brigham Young.

The Mormons had their difficulties in the West as well. Polygamy was probably part of the reason. Up until the middle of the 20th Century, every petitioner for degrees in a Utah lodge was required to list the fraternal and religious bodies to which he belonged. Dozens of prominent Freemasons within and without Utah found no reasons whatsoever for Mormons to be excluded from Freemasonry. In 1984, the Grand Lodge of Utah wisely lifted the ban on Mormon membership. Today many Mormons are leaders in Utah lodges as many were in other jurisdictions.

Prince Hall Freemasonry

The United Grand Lodge of England made an historical announcement on December 14, 1994 when it declared that the "Prince Hall Grand Lodge of Massachusetts should now be accepted as regular and recognized." It noted that all Prince Hall Grand Lodges are descended from what is now the Prince Hall Grand Lodge of Massachusetts. Thus, a two century transgression and controversy was finally corrected.

On March 6, 1775 a man named Prince Hall and fourteen other men of color were initiated into Freemasonry by Sergeant John Batt of the Irish Military Lodge No. 441, attached to the 38th Foot of the British Army near Boston, Massachusetts. On September 29, 1784 a warrant was granted the group of 15 men into African Lodge No. 459 on the English Register. This warrant is still in existence.

The Lodge contributed to the Charity Fund in England until 1797 and was in correspondence with the Grand Secretary until the early 19th century when correspondence on both sides seemed to have been ignored or lost due to the effect of transportation with North America because of the Napoleonic War.

In 1797, African Lodge, not having had a response from the Grand Lodge in England, contrary to the terms of its warrant and the English Book of Constitutions by which it was bound, gave authority to two groups of men to meet as lodges: African Lodge in Philadelphia, Pennsylvania and Hiram Lodge in Providence, Rhode Island.

After the union of the Ancient and Modern Grand Lodges in England in 1813, African Lodge was omitted from the Register as were many other lodges in England and abroad. African Lodge 459 had been carried on the English Roll until 1793 when it was renumbered 370. But African Lodge 459 in America was not informed of this change. However, the lodge was not formally erased.

Prince Hall died in 1807 and was succeeded by Nero Prince, a white Russian Jew who, after two years, returned to Russia. He was succeeded by George Middleton. He was followed by Peter Lew who warranted two lodges in Philadelphia in 1811 and one in New York in 1812. In 1824, some old records and a 1784 warrant having been found, a new petition was filed with the Grand Lodge of England for recognition by Samson H. Moody, Peter Howard, John Hilton and six other blacks. In that petition, it is claimed that the nine blacks named were Royal Arch Masons. They requested authority to confer the "other four degrees" of Masonry above the first three, solicited the "Renewal of our Charter," and stated that they had not been able for several years to transmit money or hold regular communications. The Grand Lodge of England made no reply to that petition.

When the white Grand Lodge of Massachu-

READING OF THE ORIGINAL CHARTER 459

To all and every our right Worshipful & loving Brethren, we, Thomas Howard, Earl of Effingham, Lord Howard, &c. &c. &c. Acting Grand Master under the authority of His Royal Highness, Henry Frederick Duke of Cumberland &c., &c., &c., Grand Master of the Most Ancient and Honorable Society of Free and Accepted Masons sends greeting:

Know Ye, that we, at the humble petition of our right trusty and well-beloved Brethren, Prince Hall, Boston Smith, Thomas Sanderson and several other Brethren residing in Boston, New England in North America do hereby constitute the said Brethren into a regular Lodge of Free and Accepted Masons, under the title or denomination of the African Lodge, to be opened in Boston aforesaid, and do further at their said petition, hereby appoint the said Prince Hall to be Master Boston Smith, Senior Warden, and Thomas Sanderson, Junior Warden, for opening the said Lodge, and for such further time only as shall be thought proper by the Brethren thereof, it being our will that this our appointment of the above officers shall in no wise affect any future election of officers of the Lodge, but that such election shall be regulated agreeable to such by-laws of said Lodge as shall be consistent with the general laws of the society, contained in the Book of Constitution; and we hereby will and require you, the said Prince Hall, to take special care that all and every the said Brethren are or have been regularly made Masons, and that they do observe, perform, and keep all the rules and orders contained in the Book of Constitutions; and further, that you do, from time to time, cause to be entered in a book kept for that purpose, an account of your proceedings in the Lodge; together with all such rules, orders and regulations, as shall be made for the good government of the same; that in no wise you omit once in every year to send to us, or our successors, Grand Master, or to Rowland Holt, Esq., our Deputy Grand Master, for the time being an account in writing of your said proceedings, and copies of all such rules, orders, and regulations as shall be made as aforesaid, together with a list of the members of the Lodge, and such a sum of money as may suit the circumstances of the Lodge and reasonably be expected, toward the Grand Charity. Moreover, we hereby will and require you, the said Prince Hall, as soon as conveniently may be, to send an account in writing of what may be done by virtue of these presents.

Given at London, under our hand and seal of Masonry, this 29th day of September, A.L. 5784, A.D. 1784.

"By the Grand Master's Command, R. Holt, D.G.M."

"Witness Wm. White, G.S."

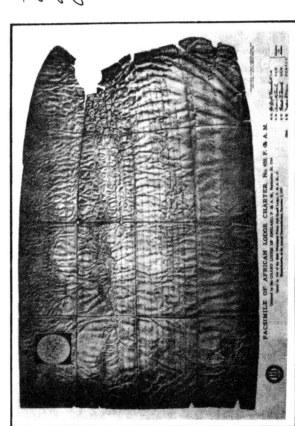

FACSIMILE OF AFRICAN LODGE CHARTER, No. 459 F. & A. M.

setts refused acknowledgment of African Lodge in 1827 and irked by no reply from England, African Lodge No. 459 declared itself to be an independent Grand Lodge and in a Boston newspaper ran such an advertisement proclaiming their independence.

In the 1830s and 1840s the new black Grand Lodge and other lodges which it had formed, made various unsuccessful attempts to form a National African Grand Lodge. The style "Prince Hall Grand Lodge" became current in the 1840s and all now use this title with the exception of *Union* Grand Lodge of Florida and *Stringer* Grand Lodge in Mississippi. All Prince Hall Grand Lodges use F. & A. M.

Schisms, however, have given rise to other groups among the blacks resulting in hundreds of black Grand Lodges calling themselves Masonic. These schisms and break-a-ways have plagued the parent Prince Hall Grand Lodge group. Offshoot bodies calling themselves Masonic have sprung up in almost every state. This has resulted in numerous law suits instituted by Prince Hall Masons in an attempt to keep its name from blemish. Prince Hall Freemasonry has been successful in these cases, particularly when recognized officials of "regular" white Freemasonry have testified in its behalf. One of the greatest stumbling blocks was, and is, the vast number of other black groups calling themselves legitimate. Serious efforts have been made to reconcile the perceived problems. At the Annual Conference of Grand Masters, papers have been presented discussing the pros and cons of blacks - one particularly, Prince Hall Masonry. While there may never be complete agreement, attempts have been increased to accommodate what differences there may be. The subject has been treated almost entirely by writers prejudiced one way or the other and it is worthy to note that as many white Masons as blacks have written books and magazine articles espousing the black cause for recognition.

Among the white supporters was William H. Upton, Past Grand Master of the Grand Lodge of Washington who wrote *Light on a Dark Subject*, later named *Negro Masonry*, in 1902. In 1898 that Grand Lodge resolved to allow Prince Hall Masons to visit its lodges. This produced a furor and the Grand Lodge reversed its position in 1899 when other white Grand Lodges threatened to sever fraternal relations. Another interesting case was that of the Grand Lodge of Massachusetts (who had objected to the 1898 Washington position) when Melvin M. Johnson, Past Grand Master of Massachusetts, in 1947, suddenly adopted the report of a committee to the effect that black Freemasonry of Prince Hall affiliation was regular and legitimate, as much so as the Grand Lodge of Massachusetts, itself. This caused some states to sever relations. Massachusetts rescinded its former resolution. It is to be observed that the Grand Lodge of Massachusetts did not repudiate its previous findings of fact or conclusions of law as expressed in 1947, but reversed its action solely in the interest of harmony.

(Note: It is interesting to note that the United Grand Lodge of England consulted the Grand Lodge of Massachusetts before they made their announcement of December 14, 1994. Massachusetts gave their hearty support for the recognition.)

Other white Masons who have supported the cause for recognition are: Harold V. B. Voorhis, 33° of New Jersey who wrote *History of Negro Masonry in the United States* in 1939, 1949; Jerry Masengill of Iowa; Christopher Haffner of England; George Draffen of Scotland; and Allen E. Roberts, foremost Masonic author of Virginia who wrote many articles for magazines, gave addresses and ignited the flame in his address* of February 22, 1989 at the Conference of Grand Masters. The matter of recognition for Prince Hall Masonry which had been simmering on the back burner for years suddenly moved to the front and the Grand Lodge of Con-

*This address has been printed in Roberts' book *The Mystic Tie,* (MACOY)

necticut was the first white Grand Lodge to declare the Prince Hall Grand Lodge of Connecticut as equal. Many other state Grand Lodges have since followed in doing so.

Among some of the black Masonic stalwart supporters have been George W. Crawford of Connecticut; Harry E. Davis of Ohio who wrote *A History of Freemasonry among Negro America*, 1946; Charles H. Wesley, *Prince Hall: Life and Legacy*, 1977; Harry A. Williamson of New York, *Prince Hall Primer*, 1925, 1956, 1959; Joseph A. Walkes of Missouri, *Black Square and Compass: 200 Years of Prince Hall Freemasonry* and *Prince Hall Masonic Quiz Book*.

The Prince Hall affiliation maintains Grand Lodges in all states. The appurtenant Masonic bodies have likewise been copied so that the blacks have Chapters of Royal Arch Masons, Councils of Royal and Select Masters, Commanderies of Knights Templar, Consistories of the Scottish Rite and the Shrine, as well as orders of the Eastern Star, Heroines of Jericho, Amaranth and Daughters of Isis for the women.

CHAPTER IX

What Is Freemasonry?

Difficulties of the Question

NOBODY knows what Freemasonry is, or, if that statement be deemed too strong, at least no one has been able to demonstrate that he knows the answer to the question. What one asserts another of apparently equal ability doubts or denies. Though different persons agree upon some phases or points of the subject, few will be able to agree upon all. Nor is this divergence of opinion due to ignorance or lack of investigation, for conflicts arise principally amongst the most zealous and erudite of Masonic students. The Fraternity has no central authority to declare its creed and no censor of books to check aberrations. Anyone, either within or without the Society, may speak or write about it what he wills, and many have taken advantage of that liberty. The wildest fancy as well as the ablest historiographic talent has swollen the volume of its literature.

Definition of Freemasonry in simple but comprehensive language has seldom been attempted, but many assertions, incomplete or misleading, and many dissertations, extended and confusing, have issued in great numbers. The bane of Masonic literature has been the tendency of so many to start with an assumed state of facts or a prejudiced notion and then to push forward to a corresponding conclusion, ignoring other factors inconsistent with it.

Many repeat unanalytically such statements as that "Freemasonry is a beautiful system of morality, veiled in allegory and illustrated by symbols," and "Freemasonry is a progressive science, taught by degrees only," and "Freemasonry is not religion but is emphatically religion's handmaid," imagining that they have defined Freemasonry. But all of these, if true, are but aphorisms. Moreover, they are not quite true. The morality of Freemasonry is not veiled at all, but is set forth in quite clear English in the ritual, although it is illustrated by symbols. Freemasonry is not a science, and if it is progressive then a large segment of the Craft are wrong in thinking it quite fixed and permanent in its doctrine. Freemasonry is not religion, it has no creed or dogma. But what "religion's handmaid" means is very uncertain. A definition, to be such, must be mutually inclusive and exclusive, that is it must describe a thing so as to include all its characters and exclude everything that is not a character of it.

Freemasonry has spread so widely, has expanded into so many degrees, and has undergone so many changes, to say nothing of having been subjected to so many diverse interpretations, that the question: "What is Freemasonry?" must first be answered by another question: when, where, and what phase of it? Though much of Masonic doctrine has remained remarkably well fixed and stable, its laws have changed, its degrees have changed, its ceremonies have changed, and doubtless the concepts of it by its members have changed.

Landmarks

About the middle of the 19th century, there arose a widely accepted notion in the United States, though the rest of the Masonic world manifested little interest, that it was possible to name the fundamental, indispensable, and unchangeable principles of Freemasonry. Many attempts were made to do that in the form of what were called "Landmarks" or "Ancient Land-marks." But the items composing them differed as propounded by the various authors, as did also the tests or criteria by which the propositions were to be formulated or selected, and sometimes the proposals put forth by an author did not cor-respond to his own definition. Indeed, it was not agreed as to what general area the Landmarks oc-cupied or applied to or to what category they be-longed, that is, whether they were laws, written or unwritten, secrets, tenets, customs, religious concepts, ceremonies, or points in the lectures. Attempts to judge them by tests of antiquity, uni-versality, and immutability failed completely. As a result, the whole subject became hopelessly con-fused by reason of the seven principal errors or misapprehensions listed in Chapter VII.

Freemasonry and the Changing World

It is difficult to understand why so many have deemed fixation a Masonic virtue, for nothing could be more dreary than a society, private or general, which, like a stagnant pool, receives no freshening stimulus, but remains the same year after year. Modern civilization is the result of change. The advent of Christianity was a change; the Reformation was a change; the inventions of the steam locomotive and the steamship were changes; likewise the typewriter, the incandescent electric light, the radio, television, the discovery of the bacterial origin of disease, antiseptics, the progress of medicine and surgery, the discovery of America, the Constitution of the United States, the abolition of slavery; all these were changes. "There is nothing so permanent as change."

Freemasonry is, to a large extent, shaped by developments in the larger society about it and of which it is a part. Some writers treat Freemasonry as though it was a monastery and Freemasons monks and recluses, devoting their whole time and thought to the Fraternity. But Freemasons are busily engaged in many occupations and undertakings in which they are more absorbed than they are in Freemasonry, because those things are more pressing and necessary for their existence. They are immersed in business, industry, and the professions by which they make their livings. They have acquired many religious, social, political, and economic ideas from their parents and from experiences of their own. It is not contemplated that membership in the Fraternity will alter these preconceived attitudes, for, whatever they may be, they are accepted as part of the candidate as he passes the ballot. So Freemasons bring ideas into the Fraternity as much as they take Masonic principles out. We have only to read the variant writings of Masonic authors to observe how differently they understand the nature of the Order.

High Degrees

Adding to the complexity of the question of what constitutes Freemasonry are some forty degrees and orders included in the York and Scottish Rites. Some say these are not a part of Masonry; others regard them as the very flower of Masonry. Some, unwilling to admit that they are "higher," call them "appurtenant," "appendant," or "coordinate," and, in modern edicts and resolutions, some Grand Lodges refer to them as "bodies confining their membership to Master Masons." It is often said that such degrees cannot be Masonic, because all Freemasonry consists of but three degrees; also that they are not higher, because they merely throw different or additional light upon or explain the three degrees. But how can anything which is not Masonic illustrate or explain that which is Masonic?

The main reasons given for excluding these additional degrees from Masonry are as follows:

First, it is said that they are not recognized by Grand Lodges, but, if that be a test, then recognition by any Grand Lodge would, to that extent, make them Masonic and so their Masonic standing might vary from time to time or from place to place. This is exactly what has occurred. In 1813 the United Grand Lodge of England recognized the "Holy Royal Arch" as a part of the third degree. In 1856, it recognized the Mark Master Degree, but reversed its action a few months later. The Grand Lodge of Scotland recognizes the Mark Master Degree, but not the Royal Arch, though it once did. The Grand Lodge of Ireland recognizes both. In the United States, neither is generally recognized, though the Grand Lodges of Colorado, Delaware, Idaho, Iowa, Massachusetts, Nebraska, New Hampshire, North Carolina, and North Dakota treat the Royal Arch, Royal and Select Masters, Knights Templar, and Scottish Rite as Masonic. Delaware seems to recognize the Order of DeMolay and various Masonic clubs, while Nebraska apparently adds the Eastern Star, Mystic Shrine, Red Cross of Constantine, National Federated Crafts, Allied Masonic Degrees, and National Sojourners. Scandinavian Grand Lodges, which confer seven or eight degrees adopted from the Scottish Rite, are nevertheless recognized as Masonic by the Grand Lodge of England and by practically all Grand Lodges in this country.

Secondly, it is asserted that Freemasonry has

always consisted of the three degrees and no more, and that an ancient Landmark forbids any change in that situation. But the most ancient Landmark on the subject, that is, in the pre Grand Lodge era, seems to establish a single ceremony as sufficient to make a man a Mason. The next oldest Landmark, the *Constitutions of 1723*, recognized only a two-degree system. A third degree is not mentioned in the records of the Grand Lodge of England until 1725, and that degree was not provided for in the *Constitutions* until 1738. It may even be that this addition of the Master's Degree suggested the numerous others which began to be formulated about that time.

Thirdly, it is said that, to be Masonic, a degree must relate to the Hiramic Legend or at least to the Temple of King Solomon. But the Entered Apprentice Degree does not, while the Mark Master and Most Excellent Master Degrees of the York Rite, and Secret Master, Perfect Master, Elu of the Nine, and Elu of the Fifteen in the Scottish Rite do. The officers and members of Craft lodges and of Grand Lodges are quite often officers and members of other branches of the Fraternity, and the laws, regulations, and practices of all grades are quite similar, so that it is hardly to be expected that sharp distinctions will be observed as to Masonic qualities in the one and the lack of them in the other.

Method of Enquiry

In attempting to ascertain what Freemasonry is, the only proper course is to study its history, constitutions, regulations, and ceremonies. It is misleading to follow the divergent opinions expressed by so many writers, many of whom were not very sensitive to facts. Many theories have been presented about the origin and content of Freemasonry which have never been accepted by realistic authorities or by Grand Lodges generally.

Pre-Grand Lodge Masonry

All that we know about Freemasonry prior to the organization of the first Grand Lodge in 1717 is contained in the Gothic Constitutions, the minutes of several lodges in Scotland, the minutes of two English lodges, a few private writings, and several exposes, which, though published after 1717, are believed to exemplify the old catechistical rituals. The Gothic Constitutions furnish the basis, not only for many modern regulations, but for some of the Masonic obligations. Though they were designed solely for operative lodges, they began to be amended in the latter part of the 17th century as lodges received more non operative Masons. About 1670, drafts of these Constitutions appeared, containing "New Articles" applicable to "accepted" Masons. Just prior to 1717, the chief characteristics of Freemasonry were:

(1) It was the remnant of a once more eminent and influential brotherhood of operative stonemasons which had been kept alive in its later years very largely by the support of theoretic members who were attracted by its long career and honorable reputation, and also by the opportunity it afforded for social recreation.

(2) It inculcated morality, brotherhood, mutual aid and assistance, and loyalty to government.

(3) It met in lodges which assembled occasionally at the summons of the Master or by the concurrence of any five or six Masons, each lodge being governed by a Master, assisted by one or more Wardens.

(4) Members were not identified with any particular lodge, but were members of a single Fraternity, enjoying the same privileges and bearing the same obligations everywhere.

(5) The members were probably bound by a sworn obligation.

(6) Certain mental, moral, and physical qualifications were necessary for admittance.

(7) The proceedings were secret, as were certain signs and means of recognition.

(8) The lodges adhered to, and based their ceremonies upon, the old Legends and Charges, which were inculcated by lectures of catechistical and somewhat symbolical character.

(9) The Society was nominally Trinitarian Christian, but there is no indication that such was more than formal or that any religious belief was prerequisite to admittance.

(10) Feasting and drinking played a prominent part in the meetings, continuing even during the ceremonies of admitting candidates.

Changes of 1717-1723

The changes effected by the organization of the Grand Lodge between 1717 and 1723 were:

(1) A Grand Lodge, headed by a Grand Master, was formed as a central governing body, and, though its jurisdiction was at first limited to London and Westminster, it was gradually accepted by other lodges.

(2) Stated Annual and Quarterly Communications were provided for, the latter consisting of the Grand Officers and the Masters and Wardens of lodges, and the Annual Assembly and Feast being attended by all Masons, though those not

members of the Grand Lodge had no voice or vote in the proceedings, except by special permission.

(3) Authority to allow the formation of new lodges was vested in the Grand Master, and Freemasons were forbidden to form new lodges without his warrant.

(4) The Old Charges were codified into six Charges of a speculative character, following the operative Charges as closely as practicable, and extensive General Regulations were adopted making detailed provisions for the conduct of the Grand Lodge, lodges, and Masons.

(5) Lodges abandoned all pretense of regulating the building trade, but employed the working tools, tenets, and customs of the operative craft to a purely speculative or moral science.

(6) Degrees, rituals, lectures, and a legend were formulated which, however, were destined to vary and develop over many years.

(7) The Society abandoned nominal adherence to Christianity and obligated the Mason only to obey the moral law, to be good men and true or men of honor and honesty.

The Decade 1730-1740

This period witnessed some of the most epochal events in the history of Freemasonry, of which the following are the most notable:

(1) Martin Clare, in 1730 in answer to Samuel Prichard's *Masonry Dissected,* published his *Defense of Masonry* in which he elaborated on the antiquity of Freemasonry, likened it to the ancient mysteries and other old philosophies, and indicated that it was but a remnant of a once more elegant symbolism.

(2) Lodges and Provincial Grand Lodges were established in Europe and America.

(3) The Grand Lodges of Ireland and Scotland were formed in 1730 and 1736, respectively.

(4) The Chevalier Andrew Michael Ramsay, at Paris in 1737, delivered his celebrated oration or charge, purporting to trace Masonry to the Crusades, and the lodges in Europe to the returning knights and princes, and gave passing approval to the idea that Freemasonry was descended from the ancient mysteries.

(5) Dr. James Anderson issued the second edition of his *Constitutions* in 1738, which, for the first time, recognized the third degree.

(6) Pope Clement XII, in 1738 issued the first Bull against the Freemasons.

(7) The Grand Lodge changed or reversed the words in some of the degrees, which aroused some objections, but the oft-repeated assertion that a schism ensued is unsupported by evidence.

(8) At the end of this decade, the fabrication of the Hauts Grades was well under way.

To some extent, by 1740, but definitely by 1750, the Society had grown vertically and horizontally; vertically, by the addition of degrees in both Britain and Europe; and horizontally, by migration into many other lands. Within the comparatively short period of 33 years from the organization of the first Grand Lodge, the Society had changed completely to a speculative moral and social order; had altered its nominal religious affiliation; had dropped most of the Gothic Legends and developed a new one; had come under the jurisdiction of national Grand Lodges in several countries; had created the rank of Master Mason to be attained by a ceremony; had sustained the addition to itself of numerous higher degrees; and had experienced tremendous growth in numbers and popularity.

The outstanding characters of Freemasonry about 1750 were:

(1) It was a symbolic derivation from the operative Fraternity of Freemasons, basing its Constitutions and symbolism on their Charges, customs, working tools, and terminology, though it was now completely speculative, the old laws and customs having been considerably amended and, in some respects, abandoned.

(2) It still inculcated morality, brotherly love, mutual aid and assistance, and loyalty to civil government.

(3) It still met in lodges, but these had become warranted lodges meeting at fixed times and place and presided over by Masters and Wardens elected for definite terms.

(4) Members were now more identified with a particular lodge, though visitation was permitted and the rights and obligation of general membership in a common Fraternity were recognized.

(5) Initiates were bound by sworn obligations.

(6) Certain mental, moral, and physical qualifications were still required of candidates.

(7) Secrecy was maintained as before.

(8) Legends, lectures, and charges were still used, but three degrees had been formulated, including one new legend, and most of the Gothic Legends had been dropped, except for slight traces of some of them remaining in the ritual.

(9) Religious neutrality had displaced Trinitarian Christianity, though, toward the middle of the 18th century, indications of Christian doctrine began to appear, and belief in God was probably somewhat generally but unofficially accepted.

(10) Lodges were under the government of Grand Lodges in England, Ireland, and Scotland; one had probably been established in France; and the Ancient Grand Lodge of England was about to be formed. Provincial Grand

Masters had been deputed in Germany and America.

(11) There had been grafted upon the stem of Craft Masonry numerous high degrees, partly in elaboration of the Legend of the third degree, but also elaborately exemplifying a new chivalric theme, reflecting a supposed origin of the Society in the Crusades, and asserting the possession of deeper Masonic secrets.

The Period 1751-1813

Freemasonry continued to increase in complexity during the last half of the 18th century. Hauts Grades and various systems and administrations thereof multiplied; the patent system of disseminating degrees and titles was introduced; a new Grand Lodge was established in England; discord split the English Craft, and, though for different reasons, was more severe in European countries; the literature of Masonry had its beginning; the Prestonian lectures appeared; independent Grand Lodges were erected in Europe; the American Revolution resulted in the severance of control by Britain in Masonic as well as political respects. The period ended with the English Craft united by the Union of 1813. In that year, there were approximately 40 independent Grand Lodges in the world.

Freemasonry since 1813

By the opening years of the 19th century, the predominance of English speaking Freemasonry was clearly predictable. Nowhere else was there displayed that talent or knack of making things work to a desirable fruition, whether it were a political state or a private society. While European Masonry was torn by the dissentions of various bodies and rites, British and American Masons reconciled differences, absorbed higher degrees of the York Rite, and, in America, even the disorganized French Rite of Perfection was expanded into the Ancient and Accepted Scottish Rite and, in that form, returned to France.

The history of Freemasonry in the 19th and 20th centuries is one of gradual dispersion and of increases in the numbers of members, lodges, and Grand Lodges. Another development was the increase in Masonic and quasi-Masonic literature, the nature and extent of which has been discussed in Chapter II. England, France, Germany, and the United States were productive of books which treated of every possible phase of Freemasonry and many other subjects asserted to be related to Masonry. Some of these attained a considerable degree of absurdity and a number of extreme notions became associated with Freemasonry, possibly never to be entirely eradicated.

The three most notable Masonic developments of the 19th and 20th centuries were: first, the revolution in Masonic historiography which occurred largely in England between the years 1865 and 1885; secondly, the remarkable expansion of the Craft in the United States; and thirdly, the great mortality of Masonic bodies in Europe under Fascism, Nazism, and Communism.

Stability of Freemasonry

From what has been said, it must not be inferred that Freemasonry is protean, but the idea intended to be conveyed is that it is not rigid or fixed. Freemasonry has, in spite of change, remained remarkably stable, and old customs, tenets, and habits have persisted in a way and to a degree almost phenomenal, especially in view of the changes which have occurred throughout the world. There has always existed in the Society a distrust of innovations. The mistake has been in supposing this tendency due to some law, written or unwritten. It has resulted rather from the conservatism of Masons and the fact that few innovations could be suggested which seemed likely to improve upon basic and time-honored concepts. Accordingly, we find a number of principles and practices in the Fraternity today which stem from the Gothic Constitutions of four or five centuries ago.

Definition of Freemasonry in all Times and Places

From the facts which have been detailed, we can extract the following definition of Craft Masonry in all times and places: Freemasonry is an oath-bound, fraternal order of men; deriving from the mediaeval fraternity of operative Freemasons; adhering to many of their Ancient Charges, laws, customs, and legends; loyal to the civil government under which it exists; inculcating moral and social virtues by symbolic application of the working tools of the stonemasons and by allegories, lectures, and charges; the members of which are obligated to observe principles of brotherly love, equality, mutual aid and assistance, secrecy, and confidence; have secret modes of recognizing each other as Masons when abroad in the world; and meet in lodges, each governed somewhat autocratically by a Master, assisted by Wardens, where applicants, after particular enquiry into their mental, moral, and physical qualifications, are formally admitted into the Society in secret ceremonies based in part on old legends of the Craft.

Every Masonic lodge in existence or that ever has existed, so far as known, answers that description; no other order that exists or ever has existed does so.

Modern Craft Masonry

To describe more particularly Freemasonry of the 20th century, the following must be added:

In modern times, the Fraternity has spread over the civilized portions of the globe and has experienced some mutations in its organizations doctrine, and practices, so that lodges have come to be subordinate to, or constituent of Grand Lodges, presided over by Grand Masters, each sovereign within a given nation, state, or other political subdivision, and there is generally, though not universally, inculcated in, and demanded of the candidate, who ordinarily seeks admission of his own free will and accord, a belief in a Supreme Being and, less generally, in immortality of the soul, the Holy Bible or other Volume of Sacred Law being displayed in the lodge and used for the obligation of the candidate during his conduction through the three degrees of Entered Apprentice, Fellow Craft, and Master Mason, the last named including the legend of King

Solomon's Temple and Hiram Abif, though additional degrees and ceremonies are not found objectionable in some jurisdictions.

Freemasonry in its Broadest Sense

Freemasonry, in its broadest and most common comprehensive sense, is a system of morality and social ethics, and a philosophy of life, all of simple and fundamental character, incorporating a broad humanitarianism, and, though treating life as a practical experience, subordinates the material to the spiritual; it is without a creed, being of no sect but finding truth in all; it is moral but not pharisaic; it demands sanity rather than sanctity; it is tolerant but not supine; it seeks truth but does not define truth; it urges its votaries to think but does not tell them what to think; it despises ignorance but does not proscribe the ignorant; it fosters education but proposes no curriculum; it espouses political liberty and the dignity of man but has no platform or propaganda; it believes in the nobility and usefulness of life; it is modest and not militant; it is moderate, universal, and so liberal as to permit each individual to form and express his own opinion, even as to what Freemasonry is or ought to be, and invites him to improve it if he can.

FINIS

232

Bibliography

BEDE, ELBERT. *The Landmarks of Freemasonry*. New York:Macoy Publishing and Masonic Supply Co., 1954.

CALCOTT, WELLINS. *A Candid Disquisition of the Principles and Practices of the Most Ancient and Honorable Society of Free and Accepted Masons*. London: James Dixwell, 1769.

DARRAH, DELMAR D. *Evolution of Freemasonry*. Bloomington, Ill.: Masonic Publishing Co., 1920.

DAVIS HARRY E. *History of Freemasonry among Negroes in America*. Philadelphia: Prince Hall Scottish Rite, 1946.

DENSLOW, RAY V. *The Masonic Conservators*. G. L. of Missouri, 1931.

FORT, GEORGE F. *Critical Enquiry into Conditions of the Constitutional Builders and their Relation to Secular Guilds of the Middle Ages*. New York, 1884.

_____ . *The Early History and Antiquities of Freemasonry, as Connected with Ancient Norse Guilds and the Oriental and Medieval Building Fraternities*. Philadelphia: R. Ball, 1877.

_____ . *Historical Treatise on Early Builders' Marks*. Philadelphia, 1885.

GOULD, ROBERT FREKE. *Concise History of Freemasonry*. New York: Macoy, reprint, 1924. London: Gale & Polden, reprint, 1951.

_____ . *History of Freemasonry*, Amer. Ed. New York: Yorston Co., 1885-89. 4 vols.

HALL, MANLY P. *The Lost Keys of Freemasonry*. New York: Macoy, 1931.

HAYWOOD H. L. *Freemasonry and Roman Catholicism*. Chicago: Masonic History Co., 1943.

_____ . *Symbolical Masonry*. New York: Doran & Co., 1923. Kingsport:Southern Publishers, reprint, n.d.

HILLS, STANLEY M. *The Freemason's Craft.* London: Chapman & Hall, 1932.

HUGHAN, WILLIAM JAMES. "Freemasonry," in *Encyclopaedia Britannica*, 11th ed., 1911.

_____ . *Origins of the English Rite of Freemasonry; Especially in Relation to the Royal Arch Degree.* Leicester, 2nd ed., 1909.

HUNT, CHARLES CLYDE. *The Landmarks.* Cedar Rapids, Ia.: G.L. of Iowa, 1943.

_____ . *Some Thoughts on Masonic Symbolism.* New York: Macoy, 1930.

HUTCHINSON, WILLIAM. *The Spirit of Masonry.* New York: Masonic Publishing & Mfg. Co., reprint, 1867. Reprint Macoy 1903.

JOHNSON, MELVIN M. *Beginnings of Freemasonry in America.* Washington, D. C.: Masonic Service Assn., 1924. Kingsport: Southern Publishers, reprint, n.d.

JONES, BERNARD E. *Freemason's Guide and Compendium.* New York: Macoy, 1950.

KNIGHT, THOMAS A.. *The Strange Disappearance of 'William Morgan.* New York: Macoy, 1932.

KNOOP, DOUGLAS, and JONES, G. P. *The Genesis of Freemasonry.* Manchester: Manchester University Press, 1947.

_____ . *An Introduction to Freemasonry.* ibid., 1937.

_____ . *The Mediaeval Mason.* ibid., 1933.

_____ . *The Scottish Mason and the Mason Word.* ibid., 1939.

_____ . *A Short History of Freemasonry to 1730.* ibid., 1940.

KNOOP, DOUGLAS, JONES, G. P. and HAMER, DOUGLAS. *The Two Earliest Masonic MSS.*, Manchester: ManchesterUniv. Press, 1938. (Contains "Regius MS." and "Cooke MS.")

_____ . *Early Masonic Pamphlets.* ibid., 1945.

_____ . *The Early Masonic Catechisms.* ibid., 1943. (Contains exposes and supposed rituals from 1723 on.)

LOBINGIER, CHARLES S. *The Supreme Council 33°.* (Scottish Rite, Southern Jurisdiction), 1931.

MACKEY, ALBERT GALLATIN. *History of Freemasonry.* (Posthumously completed by Wm. R. Singleton.) Chicago: Masonic History Co., 1898. 7 vols.

_____ . *Lexicon of Freemasonry.* Philadelphia: Moss & Co., 1866.

_____ . *Symbolism of Freemasonry, Illustrating its Science and Philosophy, its Legends, Myths, and Symbols.* Rev. ed. by Robert I. Clegg. Chicago: Masonic History Co., 1921.

Mock, STANLEY UPTON. *The Morgan Episode.* East Aurora, N. Y.: Roycrofters, 1930.

NEWTON, JOSEPH FORT. *The Builders: A Story and Study of Freemasonry.* New York: Macoy, 1930; rev. ed., 1951.

_____ . *The Men's House.* Washington, D. C.: Mas. Serv. Assn., 1923. Reprint, Kingsport: Southern Publishers, n.d.

_____ . *Religion of Masonry.* ibid., 1927.

_____ . *Short Talks on Masonry.* Ibid. 1928.

OLIVER, George. *Discrepancies of Freemasonry.* London: Hogg & Co., 1875.

_____ . *Golden Remains of Early Masonic Writers.* London: R. Spencer, 1847. (Vol. 1 attributes *A Defense of Masonry,* 1730, by Martin Clare to Dr. James Anderson.)

_____ . *Historical Landmarks.* New York: Masonic Pub. & Mfg. Co., 1865, 2 vols.

_____ . *Revelations of a Square.* New York, 1855.

_____ . *Signs and Symbols.* New York: Macoy, 1906.

_____ . *The Symbol of Glory; Showing the Object and End of Freemasonry.* New York: Macoy, 1899.

POOLE, HERBERT and WORTS, F. R. *The "Yorkshire" Old Charges of Masons.* Leeds, 1935.

POUND, ROSCOE. *Masonic Addresses and Writings.* New York: Macoy, 1953.

_____ . *Lectures on the Philosophy of Masonry.* Anamosa: Nat. Masonic. Res. Soc., 1915. (Included in the next above complete work.)

PRESTON, WILLIAM. *Illustrations of Masonry.* London, 1772.

QUATUOR CORONATI LODGE NO. 2076. *Ars. Quatuor Coronatorum Transactions.* London.

_____ . *Quatuor Coronatorum Antigrapha.* London. (Transactions containing numerous articles and essays by various authors.)

REBOLD, EMANUEL. *General History of Freemasonry in Europe.* Cincinnati: Amer. Mas. Pub. Co., 1868.

ROBBINS, SIR ALFRED. *English Speaking Freemasonry.* London:Hazell, Watson & Viney, 1929. New York: Macoy, 1930.

SHEPHERD, SILAS H. *The Landmarks.* G. L. of Wisconsin, 1924.

SMITH GEORGE. *The Use and Abuse of Freemasonry.* New York: Macoy, reprint, 1914.

STEINBRENNER, G. W. *Origin and Early History of Freemasonry.* New York: Mas. Pub. & Mfg. Co., 1868.

STILLSON, Henry L. and HUGHAN, W. J., and others. *History of the Ancient and Honorable Fraternity of Free and Accepted Masons and Concordant Orders.* Fraternity Pub. Co., reprint, 1909.

TATSCH, J. HUGO. *Freemasonry in the Thirteen Colonies.* New York: Macoy, 1929.

VOORHIS, HAROLD VAN BUREN. *Facts for Freemasons.* New York: Macoy, 1951. Rev. ed., 1953.

_____ . *History of Negro Masonry in the United States.* New York: Emmerson, 1939; reprints, 1945, 1949.

_____ . *Masonic Organizations and Allied Degrees.* New York: Emmerson, 1953.

_____ . *Thumb-Nail Sketches on Medieval Knighthood.* New York: Macoy, 1945.

WEBB, THOMAS SMITH. *The Freemason's Monitor.* Reprint, Albany: Spencer and Webb, 1797. New York: Mas. Hist. Soc., 1899.

WILLIAMSON, HARRY A. *Prince Hall Primer.* New York: author, 1925. Rev. ed. Macoy, 1946, 1949.

COMPILATIONS:

Little Masonic Library- Washington, D. C.: Mas. Serv. Assn., 20 vols., 1924. Reprint, Kingsport, Southern Publishers, 5 vols., 1946.
(Selected subjects by various authors.)

LODGE MINUTES:

AITCHISON'S-HAVEN; ALNWICK; EDINBURGH; HAUGHFOOT; KILWINNING; YORK.

MANUSCRIPTS:

Additional MS. No. 23,202, *anon.*, 1725; Briscoe MS., London, 1724-25; Matthew Cooke MS., (15th cent.), 1861; Chetwode Crawley MS.; Edinburgh Register House MS.; Graham MS., 1726; Grand Lodge MS., 1593; Regius or Halliwell MS., (14th cent.); Sloane MS., 1659; Sloane MS., No. 3329; Trinity College MS.; Watson MS., 1687.

PAMPHLETS, EXPOSES, RITUALS, SCREEDS, ETC.

See KNOOP, JONES and HAMER *Early Masonic Pamphlets* and *The Early Masonic Catechisms.*

Index

References to the principal discussion of the subject are in italics; other references are in ordinary type.

Cabiri, 17
CAGLIOSTRO, COUNT ALESSANDRO DI, 131
CALCOTT, WELLINS, 16,179
Canada, 102
Candidate, 186, 189, 221
Candid Disquisition, A, etc., 16
Canongate and Leith Lodge, 97
Canongate Kilwinning Lodge No.2, 57, 84, 96
Capitular Rite, *See* Rite, Capitular
Catechisme des Franc-Macons, 11
Catholic Church, 80, 113, 181, 176, 195-200
Cathedrals, Gothic, 29-31
Ceremonies, *See* Degrees, Rites
CERNEAU, JOSEPH, 172-173
Ceres, Festival of, 15, 179
Changes of 1717-1723, 75-76, 222-223
Charges, Ancient or Old, *See also* Gothic Constitutions, 30-31, 38, 40, 44-50, 54, 66, 137, 146, *187, 221, 223, 225;* Amended, 191; Apprentices, 46; New Articles, 45, 67, 220; of 1723, 74, 187-188, 223
Charleston, S. C., 124, 169-170
Cheater, Lodge of, 62, 67
Chetwode Crawley MS., 89-92
Chivalric, *See* Rite, Chivalric
Christian Ministries, 186
Christianity, 16, 18, 41, 76, 114, 135, 166, 185-197, 214-215, 222, 225-226
CLARE, MARTIN, 12-13, 20, 81, 95, 178-179, 224
CLEMENT XII, 80, 113, 196, 224
Clermont, Chapter of, 116, 122
Colonies, *See* American Colonies
Colorado, 218

Comacine Masters, 22, 43
Common Judge, 92
Communication, Annual, 70, 72, 189, 222; Quarterly, 70-72, 222
Communism, 229
Compagnons, *See* French Companions
Compass and Compasses, 192
Concise History of Freemasonry, A, 34, 49, 89
Congress at Paris, Masonic, 126
Connecticut, 79, 142, 153, 166, 175
Connecticut, Grand Lodge, 212-213
Constitutions, Ancient G. L., 108; Gothic, 2, 9, 25, 28, 30, 40-51, 54, 56, 71-72, 100, 176, 220; Ireland G.L., 83, 95; of 1723, 9, 40, 71-74, 82-83, 94, 101, 126, 176, 224; of 1738, 9-10, 40, 70, 83, 95, 221, 224; of 1762, 123, 169; of 1786, 168-169
Constitutions of the Freemasons, 24
Convention, Constituent, 148; at Baltimore; 106, 190; at Paris, 126
Cooke MS., 32, 39, 41, 48
Cowan, 30, 38, 57
COWDREY, OLIVER, 202
COXE, DANIEL, 136
Craft Masonry or Rite, *See* Rite, Craft
CRAWFORD, GEORGE W., 213
CRAWLEY, CHETWODE, 89-91
Creed, 232
Critical Inquiry into Conditions of the Constitutional Builders, etc., 24
"Cross Body," 173
Crown Ale House, 69

77; Grand Lodge, Modern, 99, 104, 108, 110, 166, 206, 208-209; Grand Master of, 138, 222-223; Lodges, 25, 57-58, 67, 142, 220; Masonry in the 17th century, 52-68; in the 18th century, 69-110; Provincial, G.L. of, 146; Relations of G.L. with foreign bodies, 79-80, 114, 117, 129, 138; Scottish Rite in, 173; United G.L. of, 111, 191, 218, 227

Engraved List of Lodges, 116-117

Episcopal Church, 198

Entered Apprentice, 4, 86, 91-93, 163

Essenes, 13, 17, 21, 178

EUCLID, 21, 42

Europe, generally, 8, 68, 80, 102, 112-113, 131-183, 227, 228; Grand Lodges of, 80, 112, 116-117, 224, 229; Lodges in, 116-117, 224; Modern Masonry of, 131-133; Provincial Grand Lodges, 128

Exclusive Jurisdiction, 158

Exposes, 10-11, 20, 78, 100, 177, 187, 220

FALLOU, P. A., 23

Feast and Feasting, 70-71, 222

Fellow Craft, 87; Degree, 4, 91-93, 104, 163

FESSLER, DR. J. A., 131 Field Lodges, See Military Lodges

FINDEL, J. G., 23, 25, 180

First Lodge Boston, Mass., 79, 139

First Three Degrees, See Three Degrees

Florida, 208

FORT, GEORGE F., 24, 37

Fortitude and Old Cumberland

Lodge No. 12, 69

Four Crowned Martyrs, 47

Four Old Lodges, The, 25, 67, 69

France, generally, 15, 28, 113, 116, 119, 121, 122-127, 130-131, 133, 166, 177, 193, 230; Grand Lodges, generally, 117, 122-124, 168, 170, 178-179, 226; Grand Orient of, 126-128, 191; Lodges of, 79, 113, 117; National G.L. of, 126; National G.L. at Orient of Paris, See Grand Orient; Scottish Rite in, 125, 228

Frankfort, 117, 128

FRANKLIN, BENJAMIN, 137, 139-140, 148

FREDERICK THE GREAT, 129, 167-169

Fredericksburg Lodge, Va., 98, 138

Free, 61

Free and Accepted Mason, 70

Freemason Stripped Naked, The, 11

Freemasonry, defined, 232

Freemasonry in Its True Meaning, 23

Freemasonry in the Seventeenth Century, 24, 105

Freemasonry Traced to Its True Origin, 17, 180

Freemason's Accusation and Defense, 11

Freemason's Monitor, Webb's 105, 190

Free-Mason, Free Man, Freemason, 15, 35-88

Freestone, 35

Free Will and Accord, 3

French and Indian War, 142

French Companions, 22, 28, 32, 43

Unification of Rituals, *See* Rituals
Union Grand Lodge, (FL), 210
Union of 1813, 99, 104, *110-112,* 191,227
United Grand Lodge of England, 111, 210
United States, *See* America, *134-175,* 168, 214, 218, 228-229; Constitution of, 148-149, 155, 158, 216; Development of Freemasonry in, 153; Grand Lodges in, 127, 143, 151-153; Lodges, 139, 150; Master's Lodges, 139; Political Developments in, 155; Prov. G.L.'s and G.M.'s., 136, 139, 140-143, 146; Table of Dates, 142
Universality of Freemasonry, 194, 215, 232
Unknown Superior, 115, 130
UPTON, WILLIAM H., 209
Urania, Festivals of, 15, 179
Utah, 201-205

VAN RENSSELAER, K. H., 174
Vatican, 198
Vermont, 175
VIBERT, LIONEL, 74
Virginia, 79,142,151-153
Visitation, 226
VOGEL, PAUL J. S., 16, 21, 23, 180
Volume of Sacred Law, V. S. L., *192-194, 231*
VOORHIS, HAROLD V. B., 205, 210
V.S.L., 192, 231

WALKES, JOSEPH A., 213
Wallers, 56
WALTON, GEORGE, 148
War, 144

Warden, 163, 221-222, 226, 230
Warrant, 223, 326; of 1784
WARREN, DR. JOSEPH, 141, 147, 149, 151
Warrington, 59, 67
WASHINGTON, GEORGE, 138, 149
Washington Grand Lodge, 209-210
Watson MS., William, 49
WEBB, JOSEPH, 151
Webb-Preston Work, 106
WEBB, THOMAS SMITH, 105, 166
Webb's Monitor, 190
WEBSTER, DANIEL, 150
WESLEY, CHARLES H., 213
West Indies, 79,102,169-170
Westminster, 39, 69, 222
West Virginia, 152
WHARTON, DUKE OF, 73,79
WHIPPLE, WILLIAM, 148
WHITE, W. H., 33
WHITMER, DAVID, 202
WHITMER, JR., PETER, 202
WILLIAMSON, HARRY A., 211
WIRT, WILLIAM, 154
Wisconsin, 175
Wolfstieg's Bibliography, 7
Women, 4,163
WOODRUFF, WILFORD, 204
Word, Mason, 87, 92; True, 165
Words, 62-63, 90, 224
World, Changing, 215-216
World War I, 131,144: II, 132-133
WREN, SIR CHRISTOPHER, 22, 33, 61, 74
WYKENHAM, WILLIAM, 84
WYLIE, ROBERT, 24

YORK, DUKE OF, 130
York Lodge, 43, 58, 64, 66, 77, 81, 88, 97, 99, 120, 133, 167